MOM'S BEST
Crowd-Pleasers

MOM'S BEST
Crowd-Pleasers

101 Homestyle Recipes for Family Gatherings,

Casual Get-Togethers & Surprise Company

ANDREA CHESMAN

Storey Publishing

Edited by Margaret Sutherland

Art direction and cover design by Cynthia McFarland

Text design and production by Erin Dawson

Cover photograph by Scott Dorrance

Styling for cover photograph by Lori Dorrance

Storey books are available for special premium and promotional uses and for customized editions. For further information, please call 1-800-793-9396.

Printed in the United States by Versa Press
10 9 8 7 6 5 4 3 2 1

Library of Congress Cataloging-in-Publication Data

Chesman, Andrea.
Mom's best crowd-pleasers : 101 homestyle recipes for family gatherings, casual get-togethers & surprise company / Andrea Chesman.
    p. cm.
Includes bibliographical references and index.
ISBN-13: 978-1-58017-629-3; ISBN-10: 1-58017-629-1 (pbk. : alk. paper)
1. Entertaining. 2. Cookery. I. Title.

TX731.C5435 2006
642'.4—dc22

2006013883

Acknowledgments

I had an awful lot of fun pulling this cookbook together, thanks to some wonderful friends who regularly attend Andrea's Supper Club.

When testing crowd-pleasing recipes, leftovers are the biggest problem. So, for several months I hosted a potluck every other Sunday. I cooked five or more dishes and relied on friends to fill out the menu, taste all my recipe tests, and take home the extras. Midway through the potlucks, these friends were inspired to test their own recipes. Soon we had a regular routine: each dish was introduced to the group, with an explanation of who made it and what was special about it. We enjoyed offerings from sushi to samosas, from cheesecake made from hand-milked milk, to bread baked in a backyard brick oven. There were soups and dips, cookies and tarts, salads and squash.

Thank you for wonderful company, support, food, and dishwashing: Kathy Angier, Mary Arbuckle, Hilda Billings, Christiana Bloomfield, Alice Clark, Chris Coliander, Joanna Colwell, Win Colwell, Wren Colwell, Laurie Cox, Mac Cox, Ethan Dickinson, Seth Dickinson, Beth Duquette, Jane Eddy, Marshall Eddy, Michele Fay, Levi Fleury, Noah Fleury, Alison Joseph, Rick Klein, Schuyler Klein, Chris McGovern, Liam Mulqueen-Duquette, Mark Mulqueen, Rachel Plant, Tim Price, Paul Ralston, Millie Renaud, Eben Schumacher, Olin Schumacher, Nathan Shappy, Sarah Wesson, Su White, Aiden Warren, Eric Warren, Rowan Warren, and Miles Zwicky. Thank you, too, to all the folks who continue to make Andrea's Supper Club an on-going pleasure.

Finally, thank you to the best tasters: Richard Ruane, Rory Ruane, and Sam Chesman.

And thanks to Deborah Balmuth, Margaret Sutherland, and all the hands at Storey for making this book possible.

Contents

Preface

I have a friend whom I used to call whenever I was planning to feed a large crowd and was worried that I wouldn't have enough food.

"Judy," I'd say, "this is the menu. Do you think I have enough food?" Then I'd rattle off all the details of how much I planned to buy and what I planned to serve.

"Cut it in half," she'd say. "Then you'll have enough."

She was always right; I always planned to make more than necessary. Judy was raised in the same sort of household I was. If turkey was on the menu, our mothers would make a small beef roast in case someone didn't like turkey. If mashed potatoes were planned, they'd make rice also, "Just in case." They never served one type of pie when they knew that some people preferred apple while others preferred pumpkin.

No one ever left my mother's house hungry. They don't leave mine hungry, either, though I don't go to the same lengths to please every possible appetite. My meals are simpler (healthier, too), but that doesn't mean I don't aim to make them all crowd-pleasers.

My early years of cooking included stints of cooking for a sorority and a couple of fraternities, as I cooked my way through college and beyond. My June wedding was held at a state park, and my husband and I prepared most of the food. He brewed beer and I made an assortment of Mediterranean salads, which we stored in the cooler of friends who have a market garden. We bought wines and other drinks, hired a local bakery to make pizzas, and commissioned friends to make the cakes. We hired servers for the day of the wedding, to handle setup, serving, and cleanup. It was a wonderful and memorable occasion.

I have prepared meals for runners at our elementary school's annual 5K Ridge Run and flipped pancakes for a local library's all-you-can-eat pancake breakfast. Every month, I organize and usually bake for a monthly coffeehouse series. I live among a community of friends who turn almost every party into a potluck. Though my immediate family includes just two sons, it seems I am always feeding crowds. And I love it.

Feeding crowds is tremendously satisfying, and it can even be fun if you have a good repertoire of easy recipes to rely upon. This book is filled with recipes I've developed and experiences I have learned from over the years. It includes recipes for holiday and birthday celebrations, picnics, even backyard dining off the grill. I hope it helps to make your gatherings more fun, easy-going, and rewarding.

You Can Feed a Crowd

Does your head start spinning at the thought of feeding a crowd? Does preparing just a single dish for a large potluck feel like an overwhelming task? Don't get discouraged. Remember that only six women were responsible for the first Thanksgiving feast. They prepared all the food for 91 Native Americans and 56 settlers, and the party lasted for three days. That's a lot of cooking and pot washing, but they were sucessful, and you will be, too!

How to Handle a Crowd

Maybe it's lunchtime, and your small family has doubled because the kids have friends over to play. Maybe it's dinnertime, and the grandparents show no sign of rising from the couch. Maybe the sun is shining for the first time in weeks, calling everyone out for a picnic or a sledding party. Maybe your new flat-screen TV makes your home the inevitable location for a Super Bowl party. Whatever the reason, having friends and family over should be fun and relaxed. A shower for your sister, who is expecting her first baby, a celebration for your recently divorced brother, or a birthday party for your husband all demand your best crowd-pleasing skills, but can also be a pleasure to plan and execute.

The foods that you prepare should be fun and relaxed to complement the way most of us entertain today. The days of formal dining, linens, place cards, and monogrammed silverware are mostly relics of the past — or the subject of different books. Today's entertaining is informal and often spontaneous. It includes a lot of potluck dining, where you might be asked to bring a dish to share. So it is good to have a repertoire of fast and easy foods that you can prepare with a minimum of fuss, that are easily transported, and that hold up well on a buffet table.

Planning

When you know in advance that a crowd will be gathering, the crucial questions are: what is the occasion, and how many people will you be serving? The occasion often dictates the food. A Super Bowl party requires handheld food; a kid's birthday party requires cake; and Thanksgiving means turkey. The number of people will dictate some of the food choices — and a lot of the other planning considerations, such as whether you will have to borrow chairs, whether you will serve buffet style or sitting down, even whether you can fit everyone in your house. Many parties these days are potluck, so whether or not to plan the meal as a potluck is an important decision.

When planning your menu, consider the limits of your oven and the number of burners you possess. On Thanksgiving, after the turkey comes out of the oven there will be room to bake the stuffing and the dinner rolls, but will there also be room for the green bean casserole? Maybe you should plan on green beans amandine instead.

It helps to create the menu and the shopping list simultaneously. As long as you have your cookbooks open, or your imagination rolling, it makes sense to write down all that you will need to buy. At the same time, consider how you will prepare and serve the food, and what serving dishes and equipment are required. If you are thinking, for example, of making a large quantity of soup, consider whether you will have enough soup bowls. If not, think of something else to serve. Likewise, ice-cream pies make a terrific, easy dessert for crowds, but don't attempt them if you don't have room in the freezer.

I am particularly fond of one-dish main courses, such as a hearty stew. Add bread and salad, and you have a satisfying meal without a lot of last-minute cooking. Leaving a lot of cooking to be done right before the meal is served is generally a bad idea unless you are superorganized, have a roomy kitchen, and don't mind cooking for an audience.

Equipment and Serving Ware

Standard kitchen equipment can generally accommodate cooking for as many as ten to twelve people. Twenty is possible in most kitchens. Beyond that, you may need to buy more pots and pans. Buy the best you can afford. It's bad enough to burn dinner when it is just for your immediate family; it is far more embarrassing and distressing to burn dinner for a crowd.

If you do a lot of cooking for crowds, a 10-quart stockpot and a 6-quart heavy Dutch oven with a lid will serve you in most situations. A large roasting pan will come in handy for beef and pork roasts, double batches of lasagna, roasted vegetables, braised lamb shanks, and more. The one I rely on measures 12 inches by 17 inches. It can roast a 30-pound turkey, a large beef tenderloin, or a substantial amount of baked pasta.

Making desserts for crowds tends to involve multiple batches. You make more pies, not larger ones; more cookies, not oversized ones. So multiple cookie sheets, pie plates, and cake pans are handy. I am thankful for my sheet cake pan every time I am asked to make a cake for a school celebration or a birthday cake for a crowd. Sheet cake pans typically measure 11 by 15 inches or 12 by 18 inches. This book includes one sheet cake recipe for the 11- by 15-inch pan. When baking for a crowd, don't forget that the more choices you offer, the more your guests will eat. If all you offer at Thanksgiving is pumpkin pie, everyone will have one piece. If you offer a choice of pumpkin, apple, and pecan pie, people will ask for a small slice of each, generally adding up to more than one regular-size piece.

If you are cooking for crowds, you will also be serving to crowds, so you will have to consider whether you have enough plates, silverware, glasses, and serving dishes. Paper plates and plastic utensils are always an option but, unless you are outdoors, they are less than pleasing. If you have the storage room for the items you need, consider buying used: you may be amazed at the bargains to be had at secondhand stores, thrift shops, and tag sales. A couple of serviceable platters can be put to use for all sorts of foods, from muffins served at a brunch to crackers and cheese at a drinks party to fruit or cookies for dessert, not to mention the Thanksgiving turkey.

When hosting a potluck, figure on needing plenty of extra serving utensils; some guests will bring these (ideally along with their own serving dishes), but some will not.

The menu for a potluck is sometimes organized and sometimes not. Some hosts prefer to ensure a balanced menu by specifying on their invitations which part of the meal you should contribute. Others are willing to accept the random nature of the potluck. When I am hosting a potluck, I usually cook one or two large-scale main dishes and one or two desserts — just to have the most important bases covered — as well as provide drinks. It may be counterintuitive, but I have found that the more people are invited to a potluck, the less food there is. Not many people will contribute a main dish to a potluck unless specifically asked, and so there often is not enough food to satisfy all the hungry appetites.

Organizing

I'm a great believer in lists — or spreadsheets. There is the list of people to invite (or to expect if it is a family gathering). There's the list of cooking and serving equipment you will need to assemble. There is the menu, which is really just a list of foods to be served, and there is the shopping list. Finally, there is the task list. It is a good idea to create a timetable for the cooking chores: What can be done a few days in advance? One day in advance? Are the remaining tasks doable in the time available? If not, there is still time to rework the menu. Maybe you should consider serving fruit for dessert, or buying a tart from the local bakery. Maybe you should let the local deli make the salads. Think about when you want to have the cooking completed. Don't forget to factor in time to change your clothes and freshen up.

Before you start cooking on the day of the big meal, take a few moments to set the table and assemble the serving platters and utensils you will need (or assign these chores to someone else). Who is going to light the candles, start the music, greet the guests?

Don't forget to have fun. This is your party, after all.

1 • Finger Foods, Snacks & Drinks for All Occasions

House Salsa • Guacamole

Herbed Cheese Spread

Hot Artichoke Dip

Chopped Chicken Liver

Hot Crab Dip • Deviled Eggs

Baked Brie • Keftedhes

Green Chile Quesadillas

Old-Fashioned Limeade

Old-Fashioned Lemonade

Maple Mulled Cider

Pineapple Party Punch

Eggnog • Sun Tea

House Salsa

Every house should have a basic salsa to serve with chips. This one is mine — simple, classic, and easy to make when tomatoes are in season. When tomatoes aren't in season, use canned rather than flavorless supermarket tomatoes.

2 cups seeded and finely chopped tomatoes

¼ cup finely chopped scallions

¼ cup finely chopped fresh chile pepper, such as jalapeño

¼ cup finely chopped green or red bell pepper

2 tablespoons finely chopped fresh cilantro

1–2 tablespoons fresh lime or lemon juice

Salt and freshly ground black pepper

Sugar (optional)

Hot pepper sauce (optional)

1. Mix together the tomatoes, scallions, chile pepper, bell pepper, cilantro, and 1 tablespoon lime juice. Season to taste with salt and pepper.

2. Let sit for 15 to 30 minutes. Taste and adjust the seasoning, adding additional lime juice, salt, or pepper. A pinch of sugar may bring the flavors together. If the salsa is not hot enough, add a dash of hot pepper sauce. Serve immediately or refrigerate for up to 8 hours before serving.

MAKES 2 CUPS

Guacamole

The hardest part of making guacamole is coaxing the avocados to be at their peak when you are ready to serve them. Buy avocados two or three days before you will need them, and leave them in a paper bag at room temperature. Should the avocados be ready before you need them, put them in the refrigerator for a day or two to stop the ripening process. A perfect avocado will give slightly when pressed at the stem end. Serve with tortilla chips.

2 garlic cloves, or more if desired

1 (½-inch-thick) slice sweet onion, such as Vidalia

3 avocados, halved, pitted, and peeled

¼ cup bottled or homemade salsa (see page 10)

1 tablespoon fresh lime juice

Salt and freshly ground black pepper

1. Mince the garlic and onion in a food processor. Scrape down the sides of the bowl. Add the avocados, salsa, and lime juice, and pulse until finely chopped and well mixed. Season to taste with salt and pepper.

2. Cover and let stand for at least 30 minutes before serving, to allow the flavors to blend. Guacamole is best enjoyed on the day it is made.

MAKES ABOUT 2½ CUPS

Herbed Cheese Spread

A lovely cheese spread, easily put together in minutes, this will disappear from the table fast! Serve with crackers or a thinly sliced baguette.

4 scallions, trimmed and chopped

⅓ cup loosely packed fresh basil leaves

½ cup loosely packed fresh parsley leaves

¼ cup loosely packed fresh dill

2 garlic cloves

8 ounces cream cheese, softened

8 ounces soft, fresh goat cheese

2 tablespoons fresh lemon juice

Salt and freshly ground black pepper

Crackers or sliced baguette, to serve

1. Combine the scallions, basil, parsley, dill, and garlic in a food processor and process until finely chopped. Add the cream cheese, goat cheese, and lemon juice, and process until well mixed. Season to taste with salt and pepper.

2. Transfer to a bowl and let stand for 30 minutes to allow the flavors to blend, or refrigerate and hold for up to a day. Bring to room temperature before serving. Pass the crackers on the side.

MAKES ABOUT 3 CUPS

A VERSATILE CLASSIC   This recipe is easily multiplied — or even cut in half, and is a delicious choice for many occasions. The mild, herby cheese also works well as a spread for bagels at a brunch gathering.

Hot Artichoke Dip

A classic of Southern entertaining, this dip is perfect for potlucks when you don't have time to cook. Just buy a good loaf of French bread to go with it, and assemble the ingredients in about 5 minutes. Bake the dip while you change into your party clothes.

- 2 garlic cloves
- ¼ cup loosely packed fresh parsley leaves
- 1 (2-inch-thick) slice red or sweet Vidalia onion
- 1 (14-ounce) can artichoke hearts, drained and chopped
- 1 cup mayonnaise
- 1 cup freshly grated Parmesan cheese
- Salt and freshly ground black pepper
- 2 tablespoons dry bread crumbs
- 1 teaspoon extra-virgin olive oil

1. Preheat the oven to 350°F.

2. Combine the garlic, parsley, and onion in a food processor and process until finely chopped. Add the artichokes, mayonnaise, and Parmesan. Pulse until well mixed. Season to taste with salt and pepper. Pack into a small ovenproof crock or small casserole dish. Sprinkle with the bread crumbs and drizzle with the oil.

3. Bake for 20 minutes, until the topping is browned and the dip is hot. Serve hot.

MAKES ABOUT 2½ CUPS

Chopped Chicken Liver

This is not quite my mother's chopped liver, but it brings smiles of recognition to those who love this old-world Jewish pâtè. I often make a double batch so I can send home containers of leftovers with guests who remember it as something their mothers or grandmothers used to make. Serve it with crackers or slices of challah.

4 tablespoons canola or other vegetable oil

3 cups halved and sliced onions
(3 to 4 medium onions)

1½ pounds chicken livers, trimmed and halved
Salt and freshly ground black pepper

1 cup loosely packed fresh parsley leaves

3 large eggs, hard-cooked, peeled, and quartered

2 tablespoons dry sherry (optional)

1. Heat 3 tablespoons of the oil in a large skillet over medium heat. Add the onions and sauté until golden brown, 10 to 20 minutes. Remove from the skillet with a slotted spoon.

2. Add the remaining 1 tablespoon oil to the skillet and heat over medium heat. Add the livers and season with salt and pepper. Sauté until the livers are cooked through, about 5 minutes. Do not overcook.

3. Combine the onions, liver, and parsley in a food processor. Pulse until very finely chopped and well mixed. Add the egg and pulse until chopped and mixed in. Mix in the sherry. Taste and adjust the seasoning; it will probably need more salt and pepper than expected.

4. Cover and refrigerate for at least 1 hour before serving, to allow the flavors to blend. Bring to room temperature. Adjust the seasoning to taste before serving.

SERVES 8 TO 12

Advance Preparations

Chopped liver can be made up to 3 days in advance. It can also be frozen for up to 3 months, but some loss of flavor and texture is detectable. A splash of sherry and/or a little olive oil may be needed to restore the texture after freezing.

Hot Crab Dip

The delectable crab, having evolved in the Jurassic era, is the perfect party animal — luxurious, yet comfortable under a blanket of everyday crackers.

- 1 pound crabmeat, well drained (fresh, frozen, or canned)
- 1 egg, lightly beaten
- ⅓ cup mayonnaise
- 2 teaspoons prepared horseradish
- 1½ teaspoons Old Bay Seasoning or similar seafood seasoning
- 1 teaspoon Dijon mustard
- 1 teaspoon capers
- Salt and fresh ground black pepper
- ¼ cup cracker crumbs
- Sliced French bread, toast, or crackers, to serve

1. Preheat the oven to 350°F. Butter a 4-cup casserole dish or crock.

2. Combine the crabmeat with the egg, mayonnaise, horseradish, Old Bay seasoning, mustard, and capers. Season to taste with salt and pepper. Transfer to the prepared casserole, smooth the top, and sprinkle with the cracker crumbs.

3. Bake for 30 minutes, until hot. Serve hot, offering the bread on the side.

MAKES ABOUT 3 CUPS

Small cheer and great welcome makes a merry feast.

—WILLIAM SHAKESPEARE

Deviled Eggs

There's devilment in a dish whenever a hot spice is the main seasoning ingredient, presumably because of the connection between the devil and the heat of hell. Deviled eggs can be spicy, I suppose, but they are usually made with mild American ballpark mustard, hardly a fiery seasoning. Sometimes the only food a kid finds to eat at a potluck is the deviled eggs. They bring out the kid, not the devil, in everyone.

12 large eggs

½ cup mayonnaise

1 tablespoon yellow ballpark or Dijon mustard

2 tablespoons finely snipped fresh chives or finely chopped fresh dill

1 teaspoon Louisiana-style hot sauce, such as Frank's or Crystal

Salt and freshly ground black pepper

Paprika

1. Put the eggs in a medium saucepan and cover with cold water. Bring to a boil, covered, then turn off the heat. Leave the eggs in the hot water for 10 minutes. Immediately run under cold water until the eggs are completely cold.

2. Carefully peel the eggs and slice in half lengthwise. Remove the yolks.

3. In a food processor, combine the yolks with the mayonnaise, mustard, chives, and hot sauce. Process until smooth. Season to taste with salt and pepper.

4. Spoon the filling into the whites, mounding it slightly, or pipe the filling into the whites using a pastry bag fitted with a star tip. Sprinkle lightly with paprika to garnish.

5. Refrigerate for at least 30 minutes, and serve cold. Deviled eggs are best on the day they are made.

SERVES 12

No Recipes Needed

Quick-Fix Sour Cream Dips

You don't need a recipe for some of your favorite dips — just trust your taste buds and mix up some favorites:

- *French Onion Dip:* Mix sour cream with dried onion soup mix.

- *Blue Cheese Dip:* Mix sour cream with Roquefort cheese.

- *Horseradish-Bacon Dip:* Mix sour cream with prepared horseradish (a little goes a long way) and crumbled bacon.

Every Party Needs Nuts

"Every party needs nuts," declared a friend of mine as he scooped up a handful of pistachio nuts. He's right. A bowl of nuts in the shell provides a tasty snack for the hungry and busy work for the socially inept. Here's a list of other great foods that require no fixing on the part of the host or hostess:

- Mixed nuts, pistachio nuts (provide a bowl for the shells)

- Crackers and cheese (see No Recipe Needed: Cheese Platter, opposite)

- Chips and dip

- Tortilla chips and salsa

- Fruit platter (grapes, pineapple cubes, sliced kiwis, sliced star fruit, orange sections, berries, melon cubes)

- Fruit and cheese platter (grapes, apple slices dipped in lemon juice to prevent browning, plus assorted cheeses)

- Crudités and dip (celery sticks, carrot sticks, bell pepper strips, sliced cucumbers, radishes, cauliflower florets)

- Hummus and pita pockets, cut into small wedges

- Olives

Mediterranean Mezes

Many cities have specialty stores and restaurants that serve up Greek and Middle Eastern foods that make great mezes (appetizers). Order an assortment of stuffed grape leaves (known as dolma, dolmades, or dolmathes), hummus (a chickpea and tahini dip), baba ghanoush (an eggplant dip), marinated vegetables, olives, and pita bread.

Well-Dressed Popcorn

Whether you make popcorn on top of the stove or in a microwave, it makes a terrific party snack. Serve it plain or dress it up. The suggested amounts here work with 4 cups popcorn, popped from 1 large popcorn packet, or ⅓ cup kernels.

- *Buttered Popcorn:* Melt ¼ cup (½ stick) of butter and drizzle over the popped corn. Salt to taste.

- *Cheese Popcorn:* Add 2 ounces (½ cup) of grated dry sharp cheese to ¼ cup (½ stick) of melted butter. Pour over freshly popped corn. Salt to taste.

- *Chili Popcorn:* Drizzle the popped corn with the juice of 1 lime. Sprinkle with 1 teaspoon chili powder, ⅛ teaspoon garlic powder, and ⅛ teaspoon cayenne. Salt to taste.

- *Vermont Hippie Popcorn:* Toss hot popcorn with soy sauce or tamari to taste (1 to 2 tablespoons). Sprinkle with about ¼ cup brewer's yeast, which imparts a distinctive flavor somewhat reminiscent of cheese.

Cheese Platter

Select three to five cheeses that provide contrast in terms of flavor and texture. Serve with an assortment of crackers, baguette slices, and fruit.

- *Soft-ripened or blooming rind cheeses:* Brie, Camembert, and soft goat cheeses.

- *Semisoft cheeses:* Havarti, Italian fontina, Talleggio, and Morbière.

- *Hard cheeses:* Cheddar, Swiss, Gruyère, Manchego, Tarentaise.

- *Blue cheeses:* Roquefort, Stilton, Maytag blue.

Baked Brie

When you want the food to appear brilliant and sophisticated, this is the appetizer to make. As impressive as it is, it takes no special skills to assemble this beautiful dish. At Christmastime, the pistachios are particularly recommended for their lovely green color, which contrasts with the red of the cranberries.

1 (5-inch) wheel Brie cheese (15 ounces)

¼ cup dried cranberries

¼ cup chopped pistachios or sliced toasted almonds

2 tablespoons light or dark brown sugar

2 sheets frozen puff pastry (17 ounces), thawed

1 egg, beaten

1. Preheat the oven to 400°F. Line a baking sheet with parchment paper.

2. Using a warmed sharp knife, cut the wheel of Brie in half horizontally and separate the top half of the wheel from the bottom half. Sprinkle the bottom half evenly with the dried cranberries, pistachios, and brown sugar. Replace the top half of the Brie and press firmly to secure the stuffing.

3. Unfold the puff pastry sheets to form a 9¼- by 9½-inch rectangle. Place the Brie in the middle of the puff pastry and fold the excess pastry around the wheel. Unfold the second sheet of puff pastry. Using the Brie box as a guide, cut out a circle the same circumference as the top of the Brie. Save the trimmings for decorations. With a pastry brush, brush the egg on top of the Brie. Place the pastry circle on top and pinch the edges together to seal. Brush the top of the pastry with egg. From the pastry scraps, cut out decorations using cookie cutters or a small knife. Place on top of the egg-washed pastry. Brush the entire top side of the pastry with the egg. Transfer to the prepared baking sheet.

4. Bake for about 20 minutes, until the pastry begins to turn golden brown. Reduce the oven tempurature to 325°F and bake for another 20 minutes, until the pastry is puffed and golden.

5. Place the pastry on a large serving plate. Surround with crackers. Serve while still warm.

SERVES 12 TO 15

Potluck Pick

Surprisingly, this lovely dish transports well and holds up nicely on a buffet table.

You don't have to cook fancy or complicated masterpieces — just good food from fresh ingredients.

—JULIA CHILD

Keftedhes

Throughout the Balkans and the Middle East, meatballs are served as appetizers. Closer to home, eyes always light up when a platter of them is passed through the room. It's rare to find anyone who isn't happy to spear a toothpick into these little meat morsels.

1 onion, quartered

1 garlic clove

About 10 mint leaves

¼ cup loosely packed fresh parsley leaves

1½ pounds ground lamb

1½ teaspoons salt

¾ teaspoon black pepper

¾ cup milk

1 cup dry bread crumbs

½ cup all-purpose flour, for dredging

Olive oil, for frying

Dipping Sauce

2 cups full-fat Greek yogurt (or 1 cup plain yogurt plus 1 cup sour cream)

¼ cup finely chopped fresh mint

1 garlic clove, minced

Salt and freshly ground black pepper

1. Combine the onion, garlic, mint, and parsley in a food processor and process until finely chopped. Add the lamb, 1 teaspoon of the salt, and ½ teaspoon of the pepper, and process until well mixed. Add the milk and continue mixing until the liquid is completely absorbed. Add the bread crumbs and process to mix well.

2. Cover and refrigerate the mixture for at least 1 hour, or up to 6 hours.

3. Meanwhile, make the dipping sauce by combining the yogurt, mint, and garlic in a small bowl. Season to taste with salt and pepper. Cover and refrigerate until you are ready to serve.

4. Season the flour with the remaining ½ teaspoon salt and ¼ teaspoon pepper in a shallow bowl. Form the meat mixture into balls about 1½ inches in diameter. Roll the balls in the flour and place on a clean plate. Continue until all the meatballs are formed.

5. Heat about ¼ inch of oil in a large, heavy skillet over medium-high heat. Add a portion of the meatballs in a single layer without crowding. Fry them, turning once or twice so that all sides are browned, about 6 minutes. Remove, drain briefly on paper towels, and continue frying until all the meatballs are cooked.

6. Serve immediately or hold in a 250°F oven for up to 1 hour, to serve hot. The meatballs may also be served at room temperature.

MAKES ABOUT 36 MEATBALLS

MEATBALLS FOR A CROWD   Smaller meatballs will go further when feeding a very large crowd. They can be attractively served with toothpicks, and bite-size pieces reduce the chance of double-dipping into the delicious sauce. Smaller meatballs will take the same amount of time to cook, but they will take longer for you to form and get into and out of the skillet.

Meatballs are easier to shape if you keep your hands wet.

Green Chile Quesadillas

If you are timid about serving spicy food, tame the heat of the quesadillas by substituting green bell peppers for some of the poblanos. But don't be shy about going all the way with the poblanos, which are fairly mild chile peppers.

4 poblano chiles, or 2 poblanos and 2 green bell peppers

2 tablespoons chopped fresh cilantro (optional)

4 cups grated Monterey Jack cheese, (about 1 pound)

8 (9-inch) flour tortillas
Olive or canola oil

2 cups store-bought or homemade tomato salsa (see page 10)

1. Preheat the broiler.

2. Place the poblanos (and bell peppers, if using) on a baking sheet and broil, turning the peppers until charred on all sides, 15 to 20 minutes. Place in a paper or plastic bag, seal the bag, and let the chiles steam for 10 minutes to loosen the skins. Peel and seed the peppers. Dice the flesh.

3. Preheat the oven to 375° F.

4. Mix together the diced peppers, cilantro, if using, and cheese in a large bowl.

5. Brush four tortillas with oil. Place the tortillas, oil side down, on baking sheets. Spread one-quarter of the cheese mixture on each tortilla. Spread 1 to 2 tablespoons salsa on each. Top each with second tortilla and press down gently. Brush the top tortillas with oil.

6. Bake the quesadillas for 10 minutes. Using a metal spatula, turn each over. Continue to bake until heated through and golden, about 5 minutes longer.

7. Cut the quesadillas into wedges (a pizza wheel cutter works best). Transfer to a serving platter. The quesadillas can be stacked. Serve with the remaining salsa.

MAKES 32 PIECES

Old-Fashioned Limeade

Made-from-scratch limeade is a revelation — so fruity, so much like limes, so not like the frozen concentrated drink. Because limeade isn't as ubiquitous as lemonade on a hot summer day, it is somewhat more special.

1½ **cups sugar**

8 **cups water**

2 **cups fresh lime juice**

Thin lime slices, to garnish

1. Combine the sugar and 2 cups of the water in a small saucepan over high heat. Stir until the sugar is completely dissolved. Allow to cool to room temperature. Cover and refrigerate until chilled.

2. Stir together the chilled sugar syrup, lime juice, and remaining 6 cups water in a large pitcher. Garnish with the lime slices and serve.

SERVES 8 TO 10

FRESH LIME JUICE   Limes are more perishable than lemons and vary more in their yield. A lime will give you anywhere between 1½ and 3 tablespoons juice, so you will need anywhere from 12 to 21 limes, depending on their size and juiciness.

Old-Fashioned Lemonade

Lemonade made from fresh lemons is to lemonade made from frozen concentrate as freshly squeezed orange juice is to juice made from frozen concentrate. The flavor is soooo much better, you may never serve frozen lemonade again. When you bring out a pitcher of ice-cold homemade lemonade, it signals that you care enough for your guests to make something worthy of them.

1¾ cups sugar

8 cups water

1⅔ cups fresh lemon juice (about 9 lemons)

Thin lemon slices, to garnish

1. Combine the sugar and 2 cups of the water in a small saucepan. Bring to a boil and stir to dissolve the sugar. Allow to cool to room temperature. Cover and refrigerate until chilled.

2. Remove any seeds from the lemon juice, but leave the pulp.

3. Stir together the chilled sugar syrup, lemon juice, and remaining 6 cups water in a large pitcher. Garnish with the lemon slices and serve.

SERVES 6 TO 10

A CROWD FAVORITE You might as well multiply this recipe because there won't be any leftovers. Make this early in the day so the lemonade has time to get very cold. You can store the pitcher for several hours in the refrigerator.

Maple Mulled Cider

Apple pie in a mug — there is nothing more comforting after a long day in the cold outdoors. This is the brew to use to fill your house with an irresistible aroma when you are trying to sell it.

> 2 quarts apple cider
> ¼ cup pure maple syrup
> ¼ teaspoon freshly grated nutmeg
> 1 cinnamon stick
> 6 whole cloves

1. Combine all the ingredients in a medium saucepan and simmer for at least 30 minutes, stirring occasionally.

2. Pour into mugs and serve, leaving the cinnamon stick and cloves in the pot, if possible.

SERVES 8

Setting Up a Bar for a Crowd

How Many Beer Drinkers Have You Invited?

When you are going to serve beer, figure two to three bottles per person. A ½-barrel keg or "pony" from your favorite microbrewery is equivalent to 165 (12-ounce) bottles or cans, or enough to serve 55 to 82 people.

Stocking Up on Wine

For a party of wine drinkers, plan on stocking five (750 ml) bottles for ten people. You should get roughly five servings per bottle.

Stocking a Bar

A basic, well-stocked bar contains vodka, rum, gin, scotch, bourbon, blended whiskey, and tequila. Figure that a 750 ml bottle will yield about 16 cocktails, a liter bottle will yield 22 cocktails, and a 1.5 liter bottle will yield 39 cocktails.

Pineapple Party Punch

There is no need for complicated concoctions when it comes to punch. This punch is easy to assemble and easy to dress up with rings of ice made with pineapple and maraschino cherries, as described below. Or just serve plain and congratulate yourself for the wisdom to serve a punch that won't stain if spilled on the upholstery.

1   (64-ounce) bottle white grape juice, chilled
1   (48-ounce) can pineapple juice, chilled or frozen
1   liter ginger ale, chilled

Stir together all the ingredients in a large pitcher or punch bowl. Serve immediately.

SERVES 24

PLEASED WITH PUNCH   Does anyone own punch bowls anymore? Don't let the lack of a punch bowl discourage you from serving this party favorite. You can always mix the punch in a large pot and serve it from pitchers. Or rent or borrow a bowl.

Punches should be served very cold. Reserve some of the fruit juice mixture or carbonated beverage for an ice ring or ice cubes. To make the ice ring, half fill a Bundt pan, tube pan, or gelatin mold with the fruit juice or carbonated beverage. Freeze the ring until partially frozen. Add sliced fruit or edible flowers, then fill with additional juice or soda. Freeze until solid. Add the ice ring to the punch just before serving. You can also make a ring of frozen sherbet.

Add the carbonated portion of the punch — ginger ale, seltzer, or club soda — just before serving.

Eggnog

If you are going to serve eggnog for the holidays, it had better be home-made because the commercial products use a nutmeg flavoring that tastes like bubble gum. This recipe cooks the eggs to 170°F, just shy of the temperature that would set the eggs, but high enough to kill any bacteria. So set out this eggnog on the drinks table without any raw-egg worries.

12 egg yolks	1 cup peach or apricot brandy, or more to taste
2 cups sugar	1 teaspoon vanilla extract
6 cups milk	Freshly grated nutmeg
1 pint heavy cream	

1. Beat together the egg yolks and sugar in a medium saucepan until thick. Whisk in the milk.

2. Heat the mixture over very low heat, stirring constantly, until it reaches 170°F on an instant-read thermometer. Do not overheat or cook longer than necessary.

3. Remove from the heat and strain into a large pitcher. Stir in the cream, brandy, and vanilla. Refrigerate until thoroughly chilled.

4. Pour the eggnog into a punch bowl. Grate a little nutmeg on top and serve.

SERVES 20

EGGNOG WITH A BITE This eggnog is very lightly spiked, so everyone can enjoy a little bit without disastrous results. Set the brandy out by the punch bowl for those who would prefer more spirit.

Sun Tea

Actually, you don't need any sun at all to make iced tea. Brewing tea in cold water makes a crystal clear drink, perfect for chilling and serving cold.

½ **cup loose tea leaves**

8 **cups cold water**

Lemon wedges, for serving

Superfine sugar, for serving

1. Pour the water over the tea leaves in a large pitcher. Let stand at room temperature for 2 to 8 hours, depending on how strong a brew you desire.

2. Strain the tea into a serving pitcher; discarding the tea leaves.

3. Serve over ice, passing the lemon wedges and superfine sugar at the table.

SERVES 6 TO 8

A man hath no better thing under the sun, than to eat, and to drink, and to be merry.

—ECCLESIASTES 8:15

2 • Celebration Brunch

Mom's Quantity Pancake Mix

Baked French Toast

Scrambled Eggs Deluxe

Cheese Blintzes • Sausage-Cheese Grits

Goat Cheese Breakfast Strata

Chorizo Breakfast Strata

Broccoli Quiche

Noodle Kugel • Gravlax

Apple-Spice Muffins

Peach-Orange Muffins

Sour Cream Coffee Cake

Maple-Nut Sticky Buns

Mom's Quantity Pancake Mix

This is my house mix. I developed it when I was in charge of pancake breakfast fund-raisers for my local library. Years later, I still make it regularly and store it in a gallon-size glass jar. Having it on hand makes it possible to make pancakes quickly. This mix makes a hearty pancake that doesn't sacrifice tenderness and lightness.

Dry Mix

- 5 cups unbleached all-purpose flour
- 2½ cups whole wheat flour
- 2½ cups stone-ground yellow cornmeal
- 1½ cups sugar
- 3 tablespoons salt
- ¾ cup baking powder

Pancake Batter

(SERVES 8)

- 4 large eggs
- 6 tablespoons canola oil
- 2½ cups milk
- 3 cups Quantity Pancake Dry Mix (above)

1. To make the dry mix, combine all the ingredients in a large bowl. Mix well. Store in an airtight jar.

2. To make a batch of pancakes, preheat the oven to 200°F. Place six heatproof plates in the oven to warm, if desired.

3. Combine the eggs, oil, and milk in a large bowl and beat well. Add 3 cups dry mix and beat until smooth. Transfer to a pitcher for easy pouring.

4. Spray a well-seasoned cast-iron griddle or nonstick frying pan with nonstick cooking spray and heat over medium heat. Pour out about 3 tablespoons batter for each pancake and cook for about 1½ minutes, or until bubbles appear on the pancake's surface and the edges appear dry. Flip and cook on the other side until done. Keep warm in the oven until all the batter is cooked. Serve warm.

12 CUPS MIX, ENOUGH FOR FOUR 8-SERVING BATCHES

Crowd-Pleasing Variations

Grated apples, chopped bananas or nuts, or fresh berries can be added to the batter if you like. Frozen fruit is not recommended, because it creates uncooked pockets of batter within a cooked pancake.

For even lighter, fluffier pancakes, separate the eggs and beat the whites to form soft peaks before folding them into the batter.

A Brief History of the Pancake

Pancakes were invented thousands of years ago, when the gatherers in the hunter-gatherer set discovered that mixing grains with water and heating them on a hot rock made them taste better. Later cooks added honey and leavening, and the pancake, as we know it today, was born. The word itself comes from the German *Pfannkuchen*, which became "pancake" when it crossed the Channel in the fifteenth century. In America, pancakes have appeased hearty appetites under such names as johnnycakes, flapjacks, slapjacks, flannel cakes, hot cakes, griddle cakes, battercakes, flatcars, and sweatpads.

Baked French Toast

There's no slaving over a hot stove for this easy-to-prepare brunch favorite. Just assemble the dish the night before and pop it into the oven to bake while you make the coffee.

12 (½-inch thick) slices firm white sandwich bread

5 tablespoons butter, softened

3 large eggs

1½ cups whole milk

1 teaspoon vanilla extract

¼ teaspoon salt

¼ teaspoon freshly grated nutmeg

2 tablespoons sugar

¾ teaspoon ground cinnamon

Pure maple syrup, for serving

1. Butter a 9- by 13-inch baking dish.

2. Generously butter one side of each slice of bread and arrange buttered side up in two layers in the prepared dish, slightly squeezing the slices to fit if necessary.

3. Whisk together the eggs, milk, vanilla, salt, and nutmeg in a bowl until well combined, then pour this custard evenly over the bread. Refrigerate, covered, until the bread has absorbed all of the custard, at least 1 hour, up to overnight.

4. Preheat the oven to 350°F. Remove the soaked bread from the refrigerator.

5. Sprinkle the bread with the sugar and cinnamon. Bake until the bread is puffed and its top is golden, about 1 hour. Serve immediately, with maple syrup.

SERVES 6

Scrambled Eggs Deluxe

When a crowd gathers around the breakfast table, scrambled eggs make more sense than omelets. Have all your chopped ingredients on hand before you start cooking. Toast for a crowd is easily made under a pre-heated broiler — about 1 minute per side.

12	large eggs	1	large tomato, seeded and finely chopped
⅓	cup milk		
½	teaspoon salt	1	avocado, peeled, pitted, and cubed
⅛	teaspoon pepper		
2	tablespoons butter	2	tablespoons chopped fresh chives
4	ounces smoked salmon, lox, or gravlax (page 48), finely chopped	1	tablespoon finely chopped fresh dill

1. Beat together the eggs, milk, salt, and pepper in a medium mixing bowl until well blended.

2. Melt the butter until foamy in a large skillet over medium heat. Pour in the egg mixture. Reduce the heat to low. As the mixture begins to set on bottom and sides of the skillet, lift and fold over the eggs with a broad spatula. Continue lifting and folding until the eggs are almost set, about 10 minutes. Don't rush; long and slow cooking makes tender, creamy eggs.

3. Fold in the smoked salmon, avocado, tomato, chives, and dill. Heat the scrambled eggs through, about 1 minute more. Serve immediately.

SERVES 6

Stretching Strategy

To stretch the eggs for unexpected guests, serve them as a filling for a breakfast sandwich. Onion rolls are terrific for this purpose. Surprisingly, the eggs can be reheated in a microwave oven and served (in a roll or bun) to the sleepyheads who arrive late.

Cheese Blintzes

The French have their crêpes, the Russians their blinis, and the Jews their blintzes — crêpelike wrappers usually filled with sweetened cheese or fruit. They are ideal for serving at brunch.

Wrappers

- 12 large eggs
- ½ cup water
- ½ cup milk
- 1 cup unbleached all-purpose flour
- 4 teaspoons sugar
- 1 teaspoon baking powder
- Pinch of salt
- 3 tablespoons butter

Filling

- 2 (16-ounce) containers cottage cheese
- 6 ounces cream cheese
- ½ cup sugar
- 2 teaspoons ground cinnamon
- ¼ teaspoon freshly grated nutmeg

1. To make the wrappers, combine the eggs, water, milk, flour, sugar, baking powder, and salt in a blender and blend until smooth. Let stand for 30 minutes.

2. To begin the filling, drain the cottage cheese in a strainer for 30 minutes.

3. Melt 1 teaspoon of the butter in an 8-inch nonstick crêpe pan or skillet over medium-high heat. Pour in only enough batter to cover the bottom of the pan, tipping the pan and swirling the batter to make a very thin, even pancake. Cook until the top is set and the bottom is golden, about 1 minute. Turn the wrapper over and cook until the bottom is also golden, about 30 seconds. Transfer the wrapper to a plate. Continue making wrappers, adding 2 more teaspoons of the butter to the pan as needed, until all the batter is used, stacking the wrappers on the plate. You should have 12 wrappers.

4. To finish the filling, combine the drained cottage cheese, cream cheese, sugar, cinnamon, and nutmeg in a food processor and process until smooth.

5. To fill the blintzes, put 2 heaping tablespoons filling in the bottom third of each wrapper. Fold the bottom edge up over the filling. Fold in the sides and roll up to enclose the filling.

6. To cook the blintzes, melt the remaining 2 tablespoons butter in a large skillet over medium heat. Fry the blintzes, seam side down, three or four at a time, for 2 to 3 minutes, until golden brown. Turn and fry on the second side until golden brown, 2 to 3 minutes.

7. Serve hot. The blintzes are best freshly made. They can be held for about 30 minutes on a lightly buttered baking tray in a preheated 250°F oven.

SERVES 6

Advance Preparations

The wrappers can be made one day in advance and stored, well-covered, in the refrigerator. Filled blintzes, ready to be fried, can be refrigerated for 1 day.

Sausage-Cheese Grits

Creamy grits make satisfying comfort food — equally delicious for brunch or dinner. This recipe makes a hearty main-dish casserole. Round out the meal with a fruit salad if you are serving it at brunch, or with a green salad for dinner.

6	cups water		Salt and freshly ground black pepper
1½	cups quick-cooking grits	¾	pound bulk fresh sausage
4	cups grated Cheddar cheese, (about 1 pound)	1	tablespoon canola oil
2	tablespoons butter	1	onion, diced
¼	cup chopped pickled hot peppers	1	large green or red bell pepper, diced
4	scallions, finely chopped	4	large eggs
2	garlic cloves, minced		

1. Preheat the oven to 350°F. Butter a 9- by 13-inch baking dish.

2. Bring the water to a boil in a large, heavy saucepan. Slowly stir in the grits, then simmer, covered, stirring occasionally, for 7 minutes. Stir in 2 cups of the cheese, the butter, pickled peppers, scallions, and garlic. Season to taste with salt and pepper, and stir until the cheese is melted. Spread the mixture in the prepared baking dish.

3. Brown the sausage in a large skillet over medium heat, stirring and breaking up the lumps, about 8 minutes. With a slotted spoon, transfer the sausage to paper towels to drain.

4. Pour off the fat from the skillet and wipe clean. Add the oil to the skillet and heat over medium-high heat. Add the onion and bell pepper, and sauté until the vegetables are softened, about 3 minutes.

5. Whisk together the eggs, ½ teaspoon salt, and ¼ teaspoon black pepper in a medium-sized bowl. Stir in the sausage and the vegetables. Pour the mixture over the grits. Sprinkle with the remaining 2 cups cheese.

6. Bake for 30 to 35 minutes, or until the eggs are firm. Serve hot.

SERVES 8 TO 12

Advance Preparations

This is best served fresh out of the pan. If served at a later time, it will still taste fine, but some of the creamy goodness will be lost. You could, however, prepare the sausage and vegetables in advance. Then cook the grits and put the casserole together while the coffee brews.

Goat Cheese Breakfast Strata

Stratas are perfect for feeding breakfast and brunch crowds because they are assembled the night before and baked just before serving.

18 slices firm white bread, such as sourdough, crusts removed

8 ounces soft, fresh goat cheese, crumbled

1½ cups grated provolone (about 6 ounces)

1 red bell pepper, roasted and diced

1 bunch scallions, white and tender green parts, thinly sliced

¼ cup chopped fresh basil

6 large eggs

2½ cups whole milk

1 tablespoon Dijon mustard

1 teaspoon salt

½ teaspoon freshly ground black pepper

3 tablespoons butter, melted

1. Line the bottom of a 9- by 13-inch glass baking dish with one layer of bread, cutting some slices to fit as necessary. Sprinkle half the goat cheese and half the provolone over the bread. Sprinkle with half the scallions, half the basil, and half the roasted pepper. Top with second layer of bread. Layer the remaining goat cheese, provolone, scallions, onions, and basil on top of the bread. Cut the remaining bread into ¼-inch cubes, and sprinkle over the top.

2. Whisk together the eggs, milk, mustard, salt, and pepper in a medium bowl. Pour the egg mixture over the strata; press down on the bread with a spatula. Drizzle the melted butter over the strata. Cover and refrigerate overnight.

3. Uncover the strata and let stand at room temperature for 30 minutes.

4. Preheat the oven to 350°F.

5. Bake for about 1 hour, until the center is set and the top is golden. Cut into squares and serve.

SERVES 10

Chorizo Breakfast Strata

There are two types of chorizo. The Spanish type is dried and made from smoked pork, whereas the Mexican type is made from fresh pork and must be cooked before adding it to a recipe. If you can't find Spanish chorizo, substitute another dried, fully cooked sausage, such as linguiça.

16 slices firm white bread, such as sourdough, crusts removed	4 scallions, white and tender green parts, thinly sliced
2 cups grated Monterey Jack cheese (about 8 ounces)	6 large eggs
1 cup grated Cheddar cheese (about 4 ounces)	2½ cups whole milk
4 ounces Spanish chorizo, sliced	1 teaspoon salt
2 tablespoons canned roasted chopped chiles	½ teaspoon freshly ground black pepper
	3 tablespoons butter, melted

1. Line the bottom of a 9- by 13-inch baking dish with one layer of bread, cutting some slices to fit as necessary. Sprinkle half the Monterey Jack and half the Cheddar over the bread. Sprinkle with half the chorizo, chiles, and scallions. Top with second layer of bread. Layer the remaining cheese, chorizo, chiles, and scallions on top. Cut the remaining bread into ¼-inch cubes, and sprinkle over the top.

2. Whisk together the eggs, milk, salt, and pepper in a medium-sized bowl. Pour the egg mixture over the strata; press down on the bread with a spatula. Drizzle the melted butter over the strata. Cover and refrigerate overnight.

3. Uncover the strata and let stand at room temperature for 30 minutes.

4. Preheat the oven to 350°F.

5. Bake for about 1 hour, until the center is set. Cut into squares and serve.

SERVES 10

Broccoli Quiche

Quiches are an excellent choice for a brunch crowd. They can be made a day in advance, and reheated or served at room temperature. Refrigerated pie dough takes the fuss out of crust making. What could be easier?

1 unbaked 9- or 10-inch piecrust

2 cups chopped broccoli

1 cup grated Swiss, Gruyère, or Jarlsberg cheese (about 4 ounces)

2 tablespoons chopped red onions

2 tablespoons chopped roasted or fresh red bell pepper

2 tablespoons chopped pitted black olives

3 large eggs

Milk or cream

Salt and freshly ground black pepper

1. Preheat the oven to 425°F.

2. Fit the pie dough into a quiche pan or a 9- or 10-inch pie plate. Flute the edges. Bake the crust for 5 minutes, until lightly colored. Remove from the oven and let cool. Reduce the oven to 375°F.

3. Blanch the broccoli in a medium pot of salted boiling water for 1½ minutes, drain, and immediately plunge into cold water to stop the cooking. Drain well.

4. Sprinkle ½ cup of the cheese over the partially baked pie shell. Arrange the broccoli, onion, roasted pepper, and olives on top of the cheese.

5. Beat the eggs in a glass measuring cup. Add enough milk to make 1½ cups. Season with salt and pepper. Pour over the vegetables. Sprinkle the remaining ½ cup cheese over the quiche.

6. Bake for 30 to 35 minutes, until puffed and browned. Let stand for at least 10 minutes. Serve warm or at room temperature.

SERVES 6

Crowd-Pleasing Variations

There are some very fine refrigerated pie pastries in the supermarket. They come in flat sheets or rolls, ready to be fitted into a pie plate and baked. There are generally two crusts in the package, so you might as well double this recipe and make two quiches. You can easily vary the filling by replacing the broccoli with other blanched vegetables — asparagus, spinach, or cauliflower work well — or sautéed onions, leeks, mushrooms, or bell peppers. If you don't need the second quiche that day, it will freeze well.

One of the delights of life is eating with friends, second to that is talking about eating. And, for an unsurpassed double whammy, there is talking about eating while you are eating with friends.

— LAURIE COLWIN

Noodle Kugel

Kugel, a type of Jewish pudding, is about a thousand years old. Originally made with bread, the first kugels were plain and salty, rather than sweet. About eight hundred years ago, German cooks replaced the bread mixtures with noodles. Eventually eggs, cottage cheese, and milk were added to create a custardlike consistency. In the seventeenth century, sugar was added to the recipe, and sweetened kugels were served as either a side dish or dessert. Kugel is traditionally served at the end of Yom Kippur, when Jews who have fasted all day are looking for comfort food, and cooks are happy to serve a dish that is easy to make in advance and reheat. In fact, it makes the perfect brunch dish. It can be assembled the night before and baked just before serving.

4	large eggs	1½	teaspoons ground cinnamon
3	ounces cream cheese, softened	¼	teaspoon freshly grated nutmeg
1	(16-ounce) container small-curd cottage cheese	3	cups milk
¾	cup plus 3 tablespoons sugar	1	(12-ounce) package wide egg noodles
1	teaspoon minced lemon zest	½	cup raisins
1	teaspoon salt		

1. Butter a 9- by 13-inch baking pan.

2. Combine the eggs, cream cheese, cottage cheese, ¾ cup sugar, lemon zest, salt, ½ teaspoon of the cinnamon, and the nutmeg in a food processor and process until smooth. Transfer to a large mixing bowl and stir in the milk. Add the uncooked noodles and raisins, and stir gently to mix.

3. Spoon the noodle mixture into the prepared baking dish, cover with plastic wrap, and refrigerate overnight. Check every so often to make sure all the noodles are immersed in the liquid.

4. Preheat the oven to 350°F.

5. Uncover the kugel. Mix together the remaining 3 tablespoons sugar and 1 teaspoon cinnamon in a small bowl and sprinkle over the top. Cover with aluminum foil.

6. Bake for 35 minutes. Uncover and bake for another 40 minutes, until the kugel is firm in the center and puffed and golden on the top.

7. Cut into squares and serve hot or at room temperature.

SERVES 10 TO 12

Advance Preparations

This dish is assembled the night before — in minutes. The noodles are placed uncooked in the milky batter to soften overnight. Kugel tastes best when served right out of the oven, but it can be served reheated, and it even freezes well.

Gravlax

Gravlax is a Swedish specialty of cured salmon, flavored with dill. It's the perfect homemade alternative to lox for your next bagel brunch. The curing mixture of salt and sugar causes a chemical reaction that "cooks" the fish. It's very, very easy to make, but you need to allow the salmon to cure for a day. Start with fresh, high-quality fish.

1 cup coarse or kosher salt

1 cup sugar

2 tablespoons cracked black peppercorns

1 (2–3 pound) fresh salmon fillet (preferably center piece, with skin on)

3 bunches fresh dill, stems included, plus more to garnish

Capers, to garnish

Thin lemon slices, to garnish

1. Mix the salt, sugar, and cracked pepper in a small bowl. Place the salmon in a large glass or ceramic baking dish (you may need to cut the salmon into large pieces to fit — the larger the better). Rub a handful of the salt mixture on both sides of the salmon. Turn the salmon skin side down in the dish, and sprinkle the rest of the salt mixture on top.

2. Cover the salmon with dill. Cover with plastic wrap pressed directly upon the flesh of the fish — not over rim of the pan. Place a baking pan or a cutting board smaller than the dimensions of the baking dish on top of the fish. Set several water-filled cans inside the pan or on the board (your objective is to weight the covering so that it presses down on the fish).

3. Refrigerate for 24 hours. (If you aren't serving immediately, you can cut the fillet into smaller, more manageable pieces and wrap each piece tightly in plastic wrap. Gravlax keeps up to 6 days in the refrigerator, or up to 2 months in the freezer.)

4. To serve, remove the salmon from the dish and brush off the salt mixture and dill. Place the salmon skin side down on a clean cutting board. Using the longest, sharpest knife you have, slice the fish against the grain into the thinnest possible slices, cutting the salmon off the skin and sliding the knife to remove the fish from the skin. Taste a slice. If it is too salty, rinse the salmon under cold running water and pat dry before continuing to slice. Arrange the gravlax on a platter and garnish with capers, lemon slices, and fresh dill sprigs.

SERVES 16 TO 24

A VERSATILE CLASSIC   If you are looking for a fast, impressive hors d'oeuvre, consider making a tray of open-faced sandwiches, using cocktail rye spread with cream cheese and topped with a piece of gravlax and a sprig of dill.

Apple-Spice Muffins

If you remember your nursery rhymes, then you remember the muffin man who lives on Drury Lane. That muffin man was British, and he was most likely found on the streets at teatime during the nineteenth century, ringing his bell to attract customers to his little cakes, which were generally regarded as a vehicle for the consumption of butter. These muffins are sweet enough to be enjoyed plain, but heavenly when served warm with a pat of butter melting inside. Any good pie apple, including Golden Delicious, Jonathans, or Northern Spies, are good here.

3 cups peeled, diced apples (about 3 apples)	1 teaspoon baking soda
½ cup packed light brown sugar	1 teaspoon salt
1 teaspoon ground cinnamon	¼ teaspoon ground nutmeg
¼ teaspoon ground ginger	½ cup (1 stick) butter, softened
3 cups unbleached all-purpose flour	½ cup sugar
1 tablespoon baking powder	2 large eggs
	¼ cup buttermilk

1. Combine the apples, brown sugar, cinnamon, and ginger in a small saucepan over medium heat. Cook until the apples are soft, about 5 minutes.

2. Preheat the oven to 350°F. Butter the cups of a 12-cup muffin pan.

3. Sift together the flour, baking powder, baking soda, salt, and nutmeg.

4. Cream together the butter and sugar in a large mixing bowl. Add the eggs one at a time, beating after each addition. Beat in the buttermilk. Beat in the flour mixture until smooth. Add the apple mixture and, with a spoon or spatula, stir just enough to distribute the apples.

4. Divide the batter among the prepared muffin cups. The batter will be stiff; an ice-cream scoop does a great job of distributing it.

5. Bake the muffins for 25 to 30 minutes, until they have risen and a knife inserted in the center of one comes out clean.

6. Let the muffins cool in the pan on a wire rack for a few minutes. Turn out of the pan. Serve warm or cooled.

12 MUFFINS

MUFFIN NOTES   The recipe makes rather large muffins. If you would like smaller muffins, fill the muffin cups two-thirds full to make 18 muffins. If you have to use half of a 12-cup pan, be sure to fill the empty cups with water. Otherwise, the muffins in the half-filled pan will not bake properly. Generally, muffins are best enjoyed on the day they are made. They can be served on the second day, if stored in airtight container. After that, the loss in flavor and texture is noticeable.

Peach-Orange Muffins

Most muffins taste best the day they are made — a problem when trying to prepare in advance for a crowd or a bake sale. What to do? The orange marmalade in the batter makes these muffins especially moist, which allows them to be baked ahead. Indeed, these are better on the second day, when the flavors have had a chance to mingle.

3¼ cups unbleached all-purpose flour	1 cup sugar
4 teaspoons baking powder	2 large eggs
1 teaspoon baking soda	2 cups finely diced fresh, canned, or frozen and defrosted peeled peaches
1 teaspoon salt	
1 teaspoon ground ginger	¾ cup orange marmalade
½ cup (1 stick) butter, softened	

1. Preheat the oven to 350°F. Butter 18 muffin cups.

2. Sift together the flour, baking powder, baking soda, salt, and ginger.

3. Cream together the butter and sugar in a large mixing bowl. Add the eggs one at a time, beating after each addition. Beat in the peaches and orange marmalade. Fold in the flour mixture just until smooth; do not overmix.

4. Divide the batter among the prepared muffin cups. The batter will be stiff; an ice-cream scoop does a great job of distributing it.

5. Bake the muffins for 20 to 25 minutes, until they have risen and a knife inserted in the center of one comes out clean.

6. Let the muffins cool in the pan on a wire rack for a few minutes. Serve warm or cooled.

18 MUFFINS

Bagel and Lox Brunch

There is no easier brunch to make than one that centers on bagels and lox. Most of the work is in the shopping. The menu might include fruit salad; assorted cheeses (for those who don't like lox), cream cheese, Herbed Cheese Spread (page 12), butter for the bagels; and coffee and teas.

Set out platters of sliced tomatoes, sliced sweet or red onions, and sliced avocados for adding to the bagel sandwiches. Arrange the lox on a bed of lettuce and greens, and scatter a few onion rings and capers on top for decoration.

When calculating amounts to buy, figure 1½ bagels per person, unless you are serving other hearty main dishes. Allow about 1 ounce of cream cheese and 2 ounces of lox per bagel.

A Brief History of the Bagel

The first mention of a bagel (spelled beygl) is found in regulations posted at Cracow, Poland, in 1610. The round, chewy rolls of leavened dough that were poached in water before they were baked were made to be given as gifts to women after childbirth. The first bagel bakery in the United States outside of New York City was founded by Polish baker Harry Lender, whose sons flash-froze the bagel and did much to spread the popularity of the bagel throughout the United States.

Sour Cream Coffee Cake

The American coffee cake, raised with baking powder, not yeast, is a fairly recent invention. It is called a coffee cake not because it contains coffee, but because it is meant to be served with coffee. In older cookbooks, you may find coffee cakes are called snack cakes or crumb cakes. By whatever name, coffee cakes are generally single-layer everyday cakes served at casual gatherings. The addition of a chopped apple to the filling adds great flavor and moisture. If you like, substitute a cupful of blueberries or raspberries, or a chopped pear instead.

Dough

2 cups unbleached all-purpose flour

2 teaspoons baking powder

1 teaspoon baking soda

½ teaspoon salt

Pinch of freshly grated nutmeg

¾ cup (1½ sticks) butter, softened

1 cup granulated sugar

3 large eggs

1 teaspoon vanilla extract

1 cup sour cream

Filling and Topping

½ cup light brown sugar

2 teaspoons ground cinnamon

1 cup chopped pecans or walnuts

1 large apple, peeled and finely chopped

1. Preheat the oven to 350°F. Thoroughly grease and flour a 10-inch tube or Bundt pan. Set aside.

2. Sift together the flour, baking powder, baking soda, salt, and nutmeg. Set aside.

3. Beat the butter and sugar in a large bowl until fluffy. Add the eggs one at a time, beating well after each addition. Add the vanilla and sour cream, mixing

until smooth. Fold in the dry ingredients and beat just until blended. Do not overmix; the batter will be thick.

3. To make the filling, combine the sugar, cinnamon, and pecans in a small bowl.

4. Spoon about two-thirds of the batter into the prepared pan. Sprinkle half the pecan mixture evenly over the batter. Sprinkle the apple pieces on top. Top with the remaining batter and smooth the top. Sprinkle with the remaining pecan mixture.

5. Bake for 50 to 55 minutes, until a cake tester inserted in the center comes out clean.

6. Cool the coffee cake on a rack for 20 minutes. Turn out onto a wire rack. Serve warm or at room temperature.

SERVES 12 TO 16

To invite someone is to take charge of his happiness during the time he spends under your roof.

—JEAN-ANTHELME BRILLAT-SAVARIN

Maple-Nut Sticky Buns

A holiday tradition at my house, these buns are scrumptious and well worth the effort. You must use pure maple syrup, not maple-flavored pancake syrup, in this recipe.

Dough

- 1½ cups warm milk (110°F)
- ¼ cup granulated sugar
- 1 tablespoon active dry yeast
- 4 large eggs
- ½ cup canola oil or melted butter (1 stick)
- 1 teaspoon vanilla extract
- 2 teaspoons salt
- About 6½ cups unbleached all-purpose flour

Filling

- 1 cup finely chopped walnuts or pecans
- ½ cup packed dark brown sugar
- 1½ teaspoons ground cinnamon
- ¼ teaspoon freshly grated nutmeg
- 2 tablespoons butter
- 2 tablespoons pure maple syrup

Glaze

- ¾ cup (1½ sticks) butter
- ½ cup packed dark brown sugar
- 1 cup pure maple syrup

1. To make the dough, mix together the milk and sugar in a large bowl. Sprinkle the yeast over the milk and let stand until the yeast bubbles, about 10 minutes.

2. Whisk together the eggs, oil, vanilla, and salt in a medium bowl. Stir into the yeast mixture. Add enough flour to make a smooth, soft dough, using your hands to knead in the flour when the dough becomes too stiff to stir.

3. Turn the dough out onto a floured surface and knead until the dough is springy and elastic, about 5 minutes. Place the dough in a large greased bowl, cover with a damp cloth, and let rise in a warm place until doubled in size, about 2 hours.

4. To begin the filling, mix together the nuts, brown sugar, cinnamon, and nutmeg in a small bowl.

5. To begin the glaze, melt ¼ cup of the butter and spread it generously inside a 9- by 13-inch baking pan. Sprinkle with the brown sugar and set aside.

6. Punch down the dough. Place on a lightly floured work surface and roll out with a rolling pin to form a rectangle about 12 inches by 18 inches.

7. To finish the filling, heat the 2 tablespoons butter and 2 tablespoons maple syrup together until the butter is melted. Brush onto the dough, leaving a ½-inch border on the long sides. Sprinkle the filling mixture on top, leaving a ½-inch border, and press in with the rolling pin. Roll up the dough into a tight log, starting at one of the long sides. Cut into 1½-inch slices and place cut side down in the prepared pan. Cover and let rise until it has risen about 50 percent, about 30 minutes.

8. Meanwhile, preheat the oven to 375°F.

9. Begin baking the buns. When the buns have baked for 15 minutes, finish making the glaze. Combine the remaining ½ cup butter and 1 cup maple syrup in a small saucepan. Boil for 5 minutes over medium heat. When the buns have baked for 20 to 25 minutes and the tops are golden, remove the pan from the oven and place the pan on a baking sheet (to catch the spills). Separate the buns with a spatula. Spoon the maple syrup mixture evenly over the top, allowing the syrup to flow between the buns. Return the pan to the oven for 5 minutes to caramelize the syrup.

10. Remove from the oven and immediately invert the buns onto a rimmed baking sheet. Let cool for 20 minutes before serving.

12 LARGE BUNS

Quick Cleanup

As soon as the buns are out of the pans, let the pans soak in hot water; otherwise they will be a sticky mess to clean up.

3 • Salads for Potlucks, Buffets & Picnics

All-American Potato Salad

Cheese Tortellini Pasta Salad
with Parmesan Dressing

Cold Sesame Noodles • Tabbouleh

Marinated Chickpea Salad

Thai Cabbage Salad

Marinated Vegetable Salad

Avocado and Citrus Salad

Dilled Cucumbers

All-American Potato Salad

Potato salad is a favorite at cookouts and picnics, but can be labor-intensive. You can save time by using a food processor to chop the vegetables and by cooling the potatoes in cold water, which makes the skins slip off easily.

4 pounds thin-skinned red or all-purpose potatoes

3 large celery stalks, coarsely chopped

1 red bell pepper, coarsely chopped

½ small sweet or red onion, coarsely chopped

1 cup fresh parsley leaves

3 hard-cooked eggs

1¼ cups boiled salad dressing, such as Miracle Whip, or more to taste

Salt and freshly ground black pepper

Paprika, to garnish

1. Put the potatoes into a large saucepan and fill with enough cold water to cover the potatoes by 1 inch. Bring to a simmer over medium-high heat and cook until the potatoes are tender, 15 to 30 minutes, depending on the size of the potatoes. Don't overcook. Drain well. Cover the potatoes with cold water and let cool.

2. When the potatoes are cool enough to handle, peel and slice them into ½-inch cubes. Transfer to a large mixing bowl.

3. Combine the celery, bell pepper, onion, and parsley in a food processor. Pulse just until the vegetables are chopped. Add to the potatoes in the mixing bowl. Pulse the eggs in the food processor until chopped. Add to the potatoes along with the salad dressing. Season with plenty of salt and pepper. Mix well. Add more dressing if the salad seems dry. Adjust the flavor with additional salt and pepper, if desired. Chill well. The salad will develop flavor as it sits.

4. Just before serving, taste and adjust the seasoning. Sprinkle paprika on top.

SERVES 8 TO 10

Cheese Tortellini Pasta Salad with Parmesan Dressing

Tortellini salads disappear faster from buffet tables than all other salads.

40 ounces fresh or frozen (not dried) cheese tortellini, preferably multicolored

¾ cup plus 2 tablespoons extra-virgin olive oil

8 sun-dried tomatoes

1 shallot, peeled

2 garlic cloves, peeled

½ cup freshly grated Parmesan cheese

¼ cup red wine vinegar

1 teaspoon dried oregano

½ teaspoon Dijon mustard

1 red bell pepper, cut into matchsticks

1 green bell pepper, cut into matchsticks

1 cup pitted black olives, such as kalamata

10–20 basil leaves, finely sliced

Salt and freshly ground black pepper

1. Cook the tortellini in plenty of boiling salted water until just al dente. Drain. Transfer to a large bowl, toss with 2 tablespoons of the olive oil, and refrigerate.

2. Cover the sun-dried tomatoes with boiling water and set aside to plump for 10 minutes. Drain well and thinly slice.

3. To make the dressing, combine the shallot and garlic in a blender and finely chop. Add the Parmesan, vinegar, oregano, and mustard, and process until well blended. Scrape down the blender container. With the motor running, slowly add the remaining ¾ cup oil and continue to process until well blended.

4. About 15 minutes before serving, combine the sun-dried tomatoes, bell peppers, olives, and basil with the tortellini. Add the dressing and toss carefully. Season to taste with salt and pepper.

5. Let the salad stand for about 15 minutes to blend the flavors before serving.

SERVES 6 TO 8

Cold Sesame Noodles

This salad was a big hit at my sister's wedding. I made eight pounds of noodles for that event, so feel free to expand the recipe to feed your biggest crowds. You can also add slivers of cooked chicken or shrimp for a heartier cold meal.

Salad

- 1 pound Chinese egg noodles or linguine
- 1 large head broccoli, florets cut up, stem peeled and julienned
- 2 tablespoons Asian sesame oil
- 6 scallions, trimmed and chopped
- 1 carrot, grated or shaved into curls

  Cilantro, for garnish

Dressing

- 1-inch piece fresh ginger, peeled and sliced
- 2 garlic cloves, peeled
- ¾ cup tahini
- 3 tablespoons soy sauce
- 2 tablespoons Asian sesame oil
- 2 tablespoons rice vinegar
- 2 teaspoons Asian chili paste with garlic
- 1 teaspoon sugar
- 1 cup cold, unsweetened brewed tea, vegetable or chicken broth, or water, or more as needed

1. Bring a large pot of salted water to a boil. Add the noodles and check the timing for cooking until al dente. About 3 minutes before the noodles are done, add the broccoli. When the noodles are al dente, drain them and the broccoli well. Rinse until cool under running water. Add the sesame oil and toss.

2. Combine noodles and broccoli in a large mixing bowl with the scallions and carrot. Toss well.

3. To make the dressing, combine the ginger and garlic in a blender and process until finely chopped. Add the tahini, soy sauce, sesame oil, vinegar, chili paste, and sugar. Process until smooth. Add enough tea to thin the dressing to the consistency of cream.

4. Pour the dressing over the noodles and vegetables and toss well. Garnish with a sprinkling of cilantro. Serve at once.

SERVES 6 TO 8

Advance Preparations

Like all pasta salads, this is best if served immediately after preparing. If you must make it in advance, refrigerate the noodles and vegetables separately from the dressing. The dressing will thicken on standing. Have additional cold, unsweetened brewed tea or water available for thinning the dressing as needed.

Perfect Picnics

There are many, many good reasons to make your next summer gathering an informal picnic — not the least of which is that it spares you the need to clean your house, worry about fitting too many people into too small a space, or provide entertainment for the kids.

The best picnics are kept simple, with foods that don't require a lot of last-minute preparation. Finger foods are an excellent solution for picnics and provide a good range of choices. Instead of packing premade sandwiches, consider a selection of meats and cheeses, rolls, and condiments. Salads dressed in vinegar-based marinades can be prepared the day before, hold up well even in the heat, and continue to take on a wonderful flavor over time.

When packing up to go to the picnic, make a list of every food and utensil you will need. Check off each item as you pack it to ensure that you do not forget an essential item. Pack the foods that are to be eaten last at the bottom of your cooler, basket, or backpack so you do not have to unpack everything once you start the meal. Organization is key to planning the perfect picnic.

Make sure your list includes plates, flatware, napkins, glasses, salt and pepper shakers, wine bottle openers, sharp knives, and cutting boards. A quality picnic blanket can make all the difference in your comfort while picnicking, and also serves as a barrier against insects. Although you can use a tablecloth, quilt, or sheet, it is a good idea to have a portable, easy-to-launder picnic blanket that is ready to go at your whim.

You will also need ice or prefrozen cold packs to keep your food and beverages at the right temperature, plus paper towels or, if you are going to have sticky food on hand, premoistened towelettes, plastic bags or plastic wrap for any leftovers that will not be packed in their own container, and a plastic bag for trash.

It's not a bad idea to bring along sunscreen, hats, sunglasses and other sun protection, insect repellant, and a small first-aid kit.

Tabbouleh

From the Middle East, this parsley and bulgur salad is perfect for a picnic — it's easy to transport and holds up well on a hot summer day.

2 cups uncooked bulgur	½ Vidalia or other sweet onion, diced
4 cups boiling water	⅓ cup firmly packed chopped fresh mint leaves
3 cups quartered and thinly sliced cucumbers (peeling and seeding optional)	3 tablespoons extra-virgin olive oil
4 cups lightly packed fresh parsley, leaves only	Juice of 1½ to 2 lemons
2 to 3 ripe tomatoes, seeded and diced	Salt and freshly ground black pepper

1. Combine the bulgur and boiling water in a large bowl. Cover and let stand for 15 minutes, until the grains are tender. Drain off any excess water.

2. Add the cucumbers, parsley, tomatoes, onion, and mint to the bulgur. Toss to mix. Add the oil and toss again. Add the lemon juice and salt and pepper to taste and toss again. Let stand for at least 30 minutes before serving.

SERVES 8

Advance Preparations

If you make this salad in advance, taste again before serving. It may need moistening with a little extra olive oil or lemon juice. If the flavors have dulled, brighten up the salad with additional lemon juice and salt.

Marinated Chickpea Salad

A hearty bean salad fits the bill when you are asked to bring a vegetable dish and must travel long distances. It can withstand lack of refrigeration, which makes it good for both hot-weather travel and for picnics. And it is so easy to whip together, you will be in and out of the kitchen in minutes.

3 (19-ounce) cans chickpeas, rinsed and drained	¼ cup chopped fresh parsley
4 celery stalks, diced	2 tablespoons chopped fresh mint
1 red bell pepper, diced	¼ cup extra-virgin olive oil
½ Vidalia or other sweet onion, very finely chopped	3 tablespoons sherry vinegar or red wine vinegar
1 large carrot, grated	Salt and freshly ground black pepper

1. Combine the chickpeas, celery, bell pepper, onion, carrot, and herbs in a large bowl. In a small bowl, whisk together the oil and vinegar. Pour over the salad and let marinate for at least 20 minutes before serving.

2. The salad may be made up to 8 hours in advance. Bring to room temperature before serving.

SERVES 8

To remember a successful salad is generally to remember a successful dinner; at all events, the perfect dinner necessarily includes the perfect salad.

—GEORGE ELLWANGER,
AUTHOR OF *PLEASURES OF THE TABLE*

Thai Cabbage Salad

Bright colors and fresh, unexpected flavors enliven this coleslaw. This is one salad that won't be ignored on a buffet table.

Salad

- ½ head napa or Chinese cabbage (about 1½ pounds), thinly sliced
- ¼ head red cabbage, thinly sliced
- 1 carrot, grated
- 2 red jalapeño or Fresno chiles, minced (optional)
- 4 scallions, white and tender green parts, sliced
- ¼ cup chopped fresh cilantro
- ¼ cup chopped fresh mint
- ½ cup chopped peanuts

Dressing

- ¼ cup peanut or other vegetable oil
- 3 tablespoons rice wine vinegar
- 1½ tablespoons sugar
- 1 tablespoon Asian sesame oil
- 1 tablespoon Asian fish sauce
- 1 teaspoon Thai chili sauce or other hot pepper sauce, such as Frank's
- 1 garlic clove, minced
- 1-inch piece fresh ginger, peeled and minced
- Salt and freshly ground black pepper

1. To make the salad, combine the napa cabbage, red cabbage, carrot, chiles, scallions, cilantro, and mint in a large bowl.

2. To make the dressing, combine the peanut oil, vinegar, sugar, sesame oil, fish sauce, chili sauce, garlic, and ginger in a small bowl and whisk until well blended. Season to taste with salt and pepper.

3. Pour the dressing over the salad and toss until completely coated. Add ¼ cup of the peanuts and toss again. Taste and adjust the seasoning. Garnish with the remaining ¼ cup peanuts.

SERVES 8

Marinated Vegetable Salad

I call this super salad — substantial enough to be served as a main course, but also delicious as a side dish on a buffet. It is flexible enough to be varied, depending on what you have on hand. Diced salami makes it even more substantial; sliced radicchio or red cabbage lend additional color; blanched green beans are a nice substitute for the cauliflower. Just be sure to include some crunchy vegetables, some salty olives, some luxury crowd-pleasers such as artichokes, and dress with good olive oil and lemon juice. This salad is always a crowd-pleaser.

1	head cauliflower, broken into bite-size florets
1	red bell pepper, diced
2	celery stalks, sliced
1	large carrot, grated
1	Vidalia or other sweet onion, halved and sliced
2	cups grape or cherry tomatoes
1½	cups frozen or canned artichoke hearts (not marinated in oil), quartered
1½–2	cups cooked or canned chickpeas
1	cup pitted black olives, such as kalamata
6	tablespoons extra-virgin olive oil
5	tablespoons fresh lemon juice
	Salt and freshly ground black pepper

1. Bring a large pot of salted water to a boil. Add the cauliflower and blanch for about 3 minutes, until crisp-tender. Drain, plunge into cold water to stop the cooking, then drain well again.

2. Combine the cauliflower, bell pepper, celery, carrot, onion, tomatoes, artichokes, chickpeas, and olives in a large bowl. Add the olive oil and toss gently. Add the lemon juice and toss again. Season to taste with salt and pepper.

3. Let sit for at least 30 minutes to allow the flavors to blend. Serve immediately, or refrigerate for up to 8 hours. Serve at room temperature.

SERVES 6 AS A MAIN COURSE, 12 AS A SIDE SALAD

Potluck Pick

This is a really fine salad to toss together quickly. It is a sure hit at a potluck, where tasty vegetable dishes are often scarce. Paired up with a good bread or quality frozen pizza, it makes a quick meal for an unexpected crowd.

Tossed Salads for Crowds

A simple but colorful tossed salad can be made with a variety of lettuces and greens plus thinly sliced cucumbers, thinly sliced or grated carrots, julienned red bell peppers, and cherry tomatoes. Additional vegetables might include chopped scallions or sliced red onion, finely sliced mushrooms, and sprouts. Crumbled bacon, croutons, chopped hard-cooked eggs, or crumbled blue cheese might also be added. The trick is finding the big enough bowl and calculating quantities.

Allow 1 to 2 cups of tossed salad per person. How much will be taken depends on how many other dishes are offered and whether you have dressed the salad. A dressed salad compresses, and more will be taken.

Figure that one pound of iceberg lettuce will tear into about 10 cups, but one pound of romaine lettuce will yield about 16 cups. One pound of mesclun greens will yield 6 to 8 cups. Calculate how much lettuce and greens you need, and figure that additional vegetables will add color and texture; amounts are not terribly important.

Unwashed lettuce and other greens can be stored in a plastic bag in the refrigerator for 2 to 3 days. After they have been washed, greens should be thoroughly dried and stored between layers of paper toweling in a perforated plastic bag in the refrigerator. Washed greens will keep for 2 to 3 days. For best results, when making the salad, tear lettuce into pieces; cutting causes browning. Do not tear the greens until you are ready to assemble the salad.

To dress or not to dress; that is the question. Some people prefer their salad undressed for health reasons; some picky eaters turn their noses up at any dressing but ranch; the salad stays fresh-looking longer; leftovers can be kept for a day or so — the list is long. The reason for dressing a salad is to make it simpler — no bottles of dressing to worry about, no long waits on the buffet line while people choose and pour a salad dressing. Also, many people think a well-dressed salad (that is, a salad dressed with just the right amount of dressing and then tossed) tastes better than one that is drizzled with dressing on a plate and not tossed. To dress or not to dress; the choice is yours.

TIPS
No Recipe Needed

The Well-Dressed Salad

A classic vinaigrette is made of oil and vinegar, bound together with a touch of mustard and flavored with a little garlic or shallot or herbs. The best-quality extra-virgin olive oil and the best-quality vinegar will make all the difference. Which vinegar to use — red wine, white wine, sherry, herbal, raspberry, balsamic — depends on the salad you are dressing. All work equally well with a salad of mixed greens.

Combine ¼ cup balsamic, herbal, raspberry, red wine, sherry, or white wine vinegar, 4 peeled garlic cloves, and/or ¼ cup minced fresh herbs, and 1 to 2 teaspoons Dijon mustard in a blender. Process until finely chopped and well mixed. With the motor running, add ¾ cup extra-virgin olive oil and process until fully blended. Season to taste with salt and freshly ground black pepper. Use immediately. Makes about 1 cup.

Homemade Croutons

Cut a loaf of slightly stale Italian, French, or other white bread into ½-inch cubes. Heat a generous quantity of melted butter or extra-virgin olive oil in a large skillet. Add the bread cubes, some minced garlic, a sprinkling of dried herbs, and salt and pepper. Fry, stirring occasionally, until the cubes are crisp and golden, 20 to 30 minutes. Let the croutons cool in the pan. Store in an airtight jar at room temperature for 3 to 4 days. Figure a 1-pound loaf will yield about 5 cups of croutons.

Green Salad for Twenty-Five

You will need about six heads (4 or 5 pounds) of lettuce or greens, and about 1½ quarts of dressing.

Avocado and Citrus Salad

This beautiful salad dispels the winter blues. If you want to take it to a potluck, take the vinaigrette in one container, the undressed greens in another, and the prepared fruit in a third container.

Vinaigrette

- ¼ cup extra-virgin olive oil
- 2 tablespoons fresh lemon juice
- 1 tablespoon fresh orange juice
- 1 tablespoon honey
  Salt and freshly ground black pepper

Salad

- 2 grapefruits
- 2 navel oranges
- 6 cups arugula or watercress leaves (about 7 ounces)
- 2 cups curly endive or frisée, torn into bite-sized pieces
- 3 avocados, peeled, pitted, and sliced
- ½ small red onion, peeled and thinly sliced

1. First make the dressing. Whisk together the oil, lemon juice, orange juice, and honey. Season to taste with salt and pepper.

2. To prepare the salad, peel, quarter, and slice the grapefruits and navel oranges. The easiest way to do this is to slice off the top and bottom of each fruit. Stand the fruit on a cutting board and remove the rind in even slices using a serrated knife. Trim away any remaining pith. Quarter the fruit, then slice.

3. Combine the arugula and endive in a large salad bowl. Drizzle with half the dressing and toss to combine.

4. Add the grapefruits, oranges, avocados, and onion, and toss gently.

5. Serve at once, passing the remaining dressing at the table.

SERVES 6 TO 10

Dilled Cucumbers

Is it a pickle or a salad? It's a pickle salad, says my son, who loves this dish. Easy to make and long-keeping, this cucumber dish stands out on a table filled with potato salads and pasta salads. When I make this salad during the winter, I prefer to use long English or hothouse cucumbers that are sealed in plastic and do not require peeling. In summer, I use whatever the garden is producing, preferably small pickling cucumbers with tender skins.

¾ cup white vinegar

1 tablespoon sugar

1½ teaspoons salt

8 cups very thinly sliced cucumbers (peeled if necessary)

½ Vidalia or other sweet onion, thinly sliced

¼ cup chopped fresh dill

1. Combine the vinegar, sugar, and salt in a small saucepan or microwave container and heat just enough to completely dissolve the sugar. Let cool to room temperature.

2. Combine the cucumbers, onion, and dill with the vinegar mixture and toss gently. The cucumbers will seem dry, but the salt will draw out moisture from the cucumbers to create more brine.

3. Cover and refrigerate for no less than 30 minutes before serving. The cucumbers can be stored for at least a week in the refrigerator.

SERVES 6

4 • Potluck & Buffet Hot Side Dishes

Cuban Black Beans

Maple Baked Beans

Home-Style Green Bean Casserole

Corn Pudding

Spaghetti Squash Alfredo

Cheesy Spinach-Artichoke Squares

Classic Ratatouille

Winter Squash and Leek Gratin

Tex-Mex Vegetable Casserole

Potato Squares

Baked Rice Pilaf

Cheesy Noodle Bake

Traditional Herbed Bread Dressing

Cuban Black Beans

For the growing number of vegetarians in every crowd, consider serving beans as a hearty side dish. Everyone will enjoy these healthy, filling beans.

2 tablespoons extra-virgin olive oil

1 onion, diced

2 red bell peppers, finely diced

2 green bell peppers, finely diced

2 jalapeños, seeded and finely diced

3 (19-ounce) cans black beans, rinsed and drained (about 5 cups)

1 cup water

¼ cup dry sherry

2 teaspoons sugar

1 teaspoon dried oregano

2 bay leaves

   Salt and freshly ground black pepper

2 scallions, white and tender green parts, trimmed and finely chopped

¼ cup chopped fresh cilantro

1. Heat the oil over medium-high heat in a large saucepan. Add the onion, red peppers, and jalapeños and sauté until the onion is limp, about 3 minutes. Add the beans, water, sherry, sugar, oregano, and bay leaves. Season to taste with salt and pepper.

2. Bring to a boil, then reduce the heat and simmer until the liquid is reduced to a creamy consistency and the flavors have blended, about 30 minutes.

3. Remove the bay leaves. Stir in the scallions and cilantro. Serve hot.

SERVES 6 TO 8

Advance Preparations

This dish is easily made ahead and reheated. Add the scallions and cilantro just before serving for a lively, fresh taste.

Maple Baked Beans

Adding baking soda to the cooking water helps ensure that the bean skins will soften uniformly without splitting, particularly if you are using older beans. Keep in mind that once you add acidic ingredients, such as ketchup, the skins will soften no further.

2 cups dried navy or pea beans, soaked overnight and drained

8 cups water

1 teaspoon baking soda (optional)

1 large onion, thinly sliced

¾ cup pure maple syrup

½ cup ketchup

1 tablespoon yellow ballpark mustard

1 teaspoon ground allspice

Salt and freshly ground black pepper

1. Combine the beans and baking soda, if using, in a large pot with the water. Cover and bring to a boil. Reduce the heat and simmer, partially covered, until tender, 1 to 1½ hours. Skim off any foam that rises to the top of the pot.

2. Preheat the oven to 300°F.

3. Combine the beans, their cooking water, and the onion, maple syrup, ketchup, mustard, and allspice in a bean pot or deep baking dish and mix well. Season to taste with salt and pepper. Cover and bake for 2 to 3 hours.

4. Uncover and allow the liquid to evaporate until the beans are swimming in a sweet, thick sauce, 30 to 60 minutes. Serve hot.

SERVES 8 TO 12

Advance Preparations

Baked beans are easily made ahead and reheated. If you do plan to reheat, don't cook off the bean liquid until the final reheating. Diced and sautéed salt pork can be added to make the beans more hearty and pleasing to meat eaters, but it isn't necessary.

Home-Style Green Bean Casserole

In the '60s and '70s, Thanksgiving tables all over America were graced with casseroles made from frozen green beans, cream of mushroom soup, and canned onion rings. This version is similar, but fresh ingredients make it taste much better. The beans go in the casserole raw and emerge tender but still crunchy.

5 tablespoons butter

2 cups finely chopped mushrooms (6 to 8 ounces)

¼ cup unbleached all-purpose flour

2 cups milk

2 pounds green beans, trimmed and cut into 2-inch pieces

1 small onion, halved and sliced

Salt and freshly ground black pepper

¼ cup dry bread crumbs

¼ cup freshly grated Parmesan cheese

¼ cup finely chopped shallots (1 to 3 shallots)

1. Preheat the oven to 350°F. Butter a 9- by 13-inch baking dish.

2. Melt 4 tablespoons of the butter in a medium saucepan over medium heat. Add the mushrooms and sauté until golden, about 5 minutes. Add the flour and stir to make a paste. Whisk in the milk and bring to a boil. Cook, stirring constantly, until the the sauce is smooth. Season to taste with salt and pepper.

3. Layer the beans and onion in the baking dish, sprinkling with salt and pepper as you layer. Cover with the sauce. Sprinkle the bread crumbs, cheese, and shallots over the dish. Dot with the remaining 1 tablespoon butter.

4. Bake for 45 to 60 minutes, until the casserole is bubbling and the beans are tender. Serve hot.

SERVES 8

Corn Pudding

Also known as Indian corn pudding, or green corn pudding, this is a dish that is particularly popular in the South and Midwest, where it is a traditional Thanksgiving side dish. It holds up well on a buffet table and is easy to make, with no exotic ingredients.

- 1 red bell pepper, quartered
- 1 bunch scallions, white and tender green parts, trimmed
- 3 (10-ounce) packages frozen corn kernels, thawed
- ½ cup sugar
- 2 teaspoons salt
- ½ teaspoon freshly ground black pepper
- 2 cups milk
- 1 cup heavy or light cream
- 6 large eggs, lightly beaten
- ¼ cup unbleached all-purpose flour

1. Preheat the oven to 350°F. Butter a 9- by 13-inch baking dish.

2. Combine the bell pepper and scallions in a food processor. Pulse to finely chop. Transfer to a large bowl. Put half the corn in the food processor and pulse to chop; do not purée. Transfer to the bowl with the bell pepper and scallions. Stir in the remaining corn kernels, sugar, salt, and pepper.

3. In another bowl, whisk together the milk, cream, eggs, and flour. Stir into the corn mixture until combined well. Pour the mixture into the prepared baking dish.

4. Bake the pudding until the center is just set, about 50 minutes. Let sit for 15 minutes before serving warm.

SERVES 12 TO 15

The first governor of the Plymouth Colony, William Bradford, once said, "And sure it was God's good providence that we found this corne for we know not how else we should have done."

Spaghetti Squash Alfredo

Spaghetti squash is no substitute for spaghetti, but it does go beautifully with a creamy, garlicky Parmesan sauce. Even people who claim to hate winter squash may be converted by this luxurious dish.

1 **large spaghetti squash (about 6 pounds)**

2 **tablespoons butter**

1 **cup half-and-half**

1 **cup grated Parmesan cheese**

2 **garlic cloves, minced**

Salt and freshly ground black pepper

1. Preheat the oven to 350°F.

2. Cut the squash in half lengthwise. Scoop out and discard the seeds. Place skin side up in a baking dish and add about 1 inch of water. Bake until the skin begins to give, about 45 minutes. Drain off the water, turn the squash flesh side up, and set aside to cool slightly.

3. When the squash is cool enough to handle, scoop the flesh from its skin, using a large fork and pulling it into long strands. Place in a large mixing bowl. Combine with the butter and mix gently until the butter is completely melted. Stir in the half-and-half, Parmesan, and garlic. Season to taste with salt and pepper. Mix well.

4. Return the mixture to the baking dish or place in a large casserole dish, and bake until the cheese melts, 5 to 15 minutes Serve hot.

SERVES 10 TO 12

Advance Preparations

You can make this recipe up to a day ahead and then reheat it, covered, at 350°F for about 45 minutes when you are ready to serve.

Cheesy Spinach-Artichoke Squares

There's just barely enough cheesy custard to hold the spinach and artichokes together so they can be served in neat squares. This dish transports well and the squares look delicious and are easy to serve from a buffet table. It is also very quick and easy to prepare — an ideal party dish.

4 (10-ounce) packages frozen spinach, thawed

½ cup unbleached all-purpose flour

1 teaspoon baking powder

½ teaspoon salt

½ teaspoon pepper

¼ teaspoon ground nutmeg

3 large eggs

1 cup milk

3 cups grated Gruyêre cheese (about 12 ounces)

2 (14-ounce) cans artichokes quarters, drained

2 scallions, white and tender green parts, trimmed and finely chopped

1. Preheat the oven to 350°F. Lightly butter a 9- by 13-inch baking dish.

2. Drain the spinach in a colander, pressing out as much water as possible.

3. Stir together the flour, baking powder, salt, pepper, and nutmeg in a small bowl.

4. Beat the eggs with the milk in a large bowl. Stir in the cheese, spinach, artichokes, and scallions. Add the flour mixture; stir just until combined. Transfer to the prepared baking dish.

5. Bake for about 30 minutes, or until set.

6. Let cool for 10 minutes; slice into squares.

SERVES 10 TO 12

Classic Ratatouille

This quintessential summer vegetable stew consists of summer squash, eggplant, bell peppers, and tomatoes. The flavors are blended, yet each vegetable remains distinct. The dish is perfect for parties because it is just as tasty served at room temperature as it is served hot. It can be transported to picnics, where it makes a welcome change from salads and a special topping for veggie burgers. Feel free to make this a day or two in advance; the flavors will only improve.

7 tablespoons extra-virgin olive oil	2 small zucchini, diced
1 medium-sized eggplant, peeled and diced	2 small yellow summer squash, diced
Salt and freshly ground black pepper	2 ripe tomatoes, seeded and diced
1 onion, diced	4 garlic cloves, minced
1 small green bell pepper, diced	1 (8-ounce) can unseasoned tomato sauce or tomato purée
1 small red bell pepper, diced	

1. Heat 3 tablespoons of the oil in a large skillet over medium-high heat. Add the eggplant and season with salt and pepper. Sauté until browned, juicy, and cooked through, 10 to 12 minutes. Transfer to a medium saucepan with a slotted spoon.

2. Return the skillet to medium-high heat and add 2 more tablespoons of the oil. Add the onion and bell peppers, and sauté until tender-crisp, 3 to 5 minutes. Transfer to the saucepan with a slotted spoon.

3. Return the skillet to medium-high heat and add the remaining 2 tablespoons oil. Add the zucchini and summer squash and season with salt and pepper. Sauté until tender-crisp, 3 to 5 minutes. Transfer to the saucepan and add the tomatoes, garlic, and tomato sauce.

4. Simmer the ratatouille for 15 minutes over medium heat.

5. Taste and adjust the seasoning. You can serve immediately, but the flavor will improve if the ratatouille sits at room temperature for 1 to 2 hours. Serve at room temperature, or reheat and serve warm.

SERVES 6 TO 8

TIP

Setting Up a Buffet Table

Although there is no right or wrong way to arrange a buffet table, a logical order will make it easier for your guests. Appetizers should be served first, preferably passed on trays or arranged on the table first, then cleared away. For the meal, arrange the plates, bowls, silverware, and napkins at the head of the table. Follow with the salads. Place side dishes (cold, then hot) before the main dishes. Follow with breads and butter, if serving. The drinks should be at the end, or perhaps on a separate table. Likewise, the desserts may be set out on a separate table, brought out after the main part of the meal is finished, or arranged at the foot of the table.

Winter Squash and Leek Gratin

This is a wonderful dish to serve at Thanksgiving, if you can spare the oven space. It holds its heat well on a buffet table and doesn't require any last minute fussing.

½ cup apple cider	2 large garlic cloves, minced
1 cup sweetened dried cranberries	1 tablespoon minced fresh thyme leaves
3½–4 pounds butternut squash, peeled, seeded, and cut into ½-inch cubes	Salt and freshly ground black pepper
3 tablespoons extra-virgin olive oil	½ cup pine nuts
2 leeks, trimmed and sliced	3 tablespoons dry bread crumbs

1. Preheat the oven to 400°F. Lightly oil a 2½ quart gratin dish or 9- by 13-inch baking dish.

2. Heat the apple cider in a microwave oven until hot. Add the cranberries and set aside for at least 10 minutes.

3. Combine the squash with the oil, leeks, garlic, and thyme in a large bowl. Season with salt and pepper. Toss to coat the vegetables with the oil. Add the cranberry mixture and mix well. Transfer the mixture to the prepared gratin dish. Sprinkle evenly with the pine nuts and bread crumbs.

4. Bake until the squash is tender and top is golden, about 1 hour. If the top begins to brown too much, cover with foil. Serve hot.

SERVES 8 TO 12

Tex-Mex Vegetable Casserole

A blanket of cheese helps this dish travel well and hold its heat on a buffet table. It makes a good accompaniment to almost any main course, and is especially appreciated by vegetarians.

2   tablespoons extra-virgin olive oil

1   tablespoon chili powder

2   medium-sized zucchini or yellow summer squash, quartered lengthwise and sliced ¼-inch thick

1   small onion, diced

1   green bell pepper, diced

1   red bell pepper, diced

2   jalapeños, seeded and diced

2   garlic cloves, minced

1   (15-ounce) can diced tomatoes with juice, drained

1   (15-ounce) can pink beans or pinto beans, rinsed and drained

2   cups fresh or frozen corn kernels

¼   cup chopped fresh cilantro

Salt and freshly ground black pepper

1   cup grated Monterey Jack cheese (about 4 ounces)

1. Preheat the oven to 350°F. Lightly oil a 2½-quart casserole dish.

2. Heat the oil in a large skillet over medium-high heat. Add the chili powder, zucchini, onion, bell peppers, jalapeños, and garlic, and sauté until the vegetables are softened, about 5 minutes. Transfer the vegetables to the prepared casserole dish.

3. Stir in the tomatoes, beans, corn, and cilantro. Season to taste with salt and pepper. Top with the cheese.

4. Bake until the cheese is melted and the vegetable mixture is hot, about 30 minutes. Serve hot.

SERVES 6 TO 8

Potluck Pick

This takes very little time to prepare. It is a particularly good choice for the times you are asked to bring a vegetable dish. Leftovers can be combined with rice for an instant meal.

Potato Squares

This is my mom's potato kugel, all dressed up with cheese. It is prettier and tastier than the original, and fills in well as a satisfying vegetarian main dish. If you use thin-skinned red potatoes, peeling is not necessary. The food processor does a fast and excellent job of grating all the ingredients.

3 pounds potatoes, peeled (optional) and grated

1 onion, grated

1 carrot, grated

1 cup grated Gruyère cheese, (about 4 ounces)

½ cup cottage cheese

3 scallions, white and tender green parts, finely chopped

2 teaspoons salt

½ teaspoon black pepper

2 large eggs, lightly beaten

1. Preheat the oven to 350°F. Butter a 9- by 13-inch baking dish.

2. Combine the potatoes, onion, carrot, Gruyère, cottage cheese, scallions, salt, and pepper in a large mixing bowl. Mix in the eggs. Scrape into the prepared baking dish.

3. Bake for 1 to 1¼ hours, until the potatoes are soft. Cut into squares; serve hot.

SERVES 6 TO 8

Baked Rice Pilaf

A heavy Dutch oven easily goes from the oven to the table, and retains heat in the car and on a buffet table. Baking the pilaf also allows you to fix it and forget it — a handy thing when you are busy with other last-minute preparations.

2 tablespoons extra-virgin olive oil	¼ cup wild rice
1 onion, diced	4 cups chicken or vegetable broth
2 garlic cloves, minced	Salt and freshly ground black pepper
1 cup white long-grain rice	¼ cup chopped fresh parsley, cilantro, or basil
1 cup brown long-grain rice	

1. Preheat the oven to 350°F.

2. Heat the oil in a large Dutch oven over medium-high heat. Add the onion and garlic, and sauté until softened, 3 to 4 minutes. Add the white rice, brown rice, and wild rice, and sauté until toasted, 3 to 4 minutes.

3. Stir in the broth and bring to a boil. Cover, transfer to the oven, and bake for 35 minutes, until the rice is tender and the liquid is absorbed. Remove from the oven, mix in the parsley, and fluff with a fork. Serve immediately, or replace the cover and hold for up to a half-hour without much loss in heat or texture.

SERVES 6 TO 8

Crowd-Pleasing Variations

The recipe calls for parsley being added just before serving, to add a little flavor and color. If you are serving the rice with Middle Eastern or Mexican foods, replace the parsley with cilantro. For an Italian menu, you might want to add some basil to the parsley or use basil only.

Cheesy Noodle Bake

What do you make for a divorce party? Or for a friend with a broken heart? Why, noodles, of course, the ultimate comfort food. This is a great side dish, but you can make it a main dish by adding steamed broccoli and a salad to round out the meal.

1	pound egg noodles	¼	cup chopped fresh chives or scallions
3	tablespoons butter	½	cup sour cream
1	cup grated sharp Cheddar cheese, (about 4 ounces)	2	eggs, lightly beaten
1	(16-ounce) container small-curd cottage cheese	½	cup milk
2–4	garlic cloves, minced (optional)		Salt and freshly ground black pepper

1. Preheat the oven to 350°F. Butter a 9- by 13-inch baking dish.

2. Cook the noodles as directed on package; drain.

3. Return the noodles to the pot and stir in the butter until melted. Mix in half the Cheddar cheese, the cottage cheese, garlic, if using, and chives. In a small bowl, beat together the sour cream, eggs, and milk. Mix into the noodles. Season with salt and pepper.

3. Transfer the noodles to the baking dish and sprinkle with the remaining Cheddar cheese.

4. Bake for 20 to 30 minutes, until set. Serve hot.

SERVES 8 TO 10

GARLIC ALERT   The garlic packs a wallop because it is added raw and never fully cooks. Whether to add it and how much to add is up to you.

Traditional Herbed Bread Dressing

You call it stuffing, I call it dressing. Some people think stuffing is stuffed in a bird while dressing is baked in a casserole and served next to the bird. Whatever you call it, just make sure it accompanies the turkey you roast for the holiday. The recipe makes about 10 cups of dressing. It is essential to use high-quality bread, fresh herbs, and butter.

12 cups cubed bakery or homemade bread (about 18 slices)	1 teaspoon chopped fresh rosemary
6 tablespoons butter	1½ cups vegetable, turkey, or chicken broth
2 onions, finely chopped	3 scallions, white and tender green parts, finely chopped
3 celery stalks with leaves, finely chopped	Salt and freshly ground black pepper
3 tablespoons chopped fresh sage	
1½ tablespoons chopped fresh thyme	

1. Preheat the oven to 325°F. Butter a 9- by 13-inch baking dish.

2. Spread the bread cubes in single layers on two baking sheets and toast lightly in the oven for 5 to 10 minutes. Set aside in a large mixing bowl.

3. Melt the butter in a large skillet over medium heat. Add the onions, celery, sage, thyme, and rosemary. Sauté until the onion is translucent, about 5 minutes.

4. Transfer the sautéed mixture to the bowl with the bread cubes and toss to mix. Add the broth, scallions, and salt and pepper to taste. Transfer the mixture to the prepared baking dish. Cover with aluminum foil.

5. Bake for 15 minutes, uncover, and continue baking for 15 minutes, until the top gets a crispy crust.

SERVES 8

5 • Main Dish Crowd-Pleasers

Big-Crowd Vegetarian Chili • Pizza Party Pizzas

Spaghetti with Three Sauces • Pesto Spinach Lasagna

Big-Crowd Vegetarian Pasta Casserole

Orzo with Shrimp, Spinach, and Artichokes

Big-Crowd Pasta Casserole with Sausage

Lemon-Garlic Roast Chicken Breasts

Braised Chicken Provençale

Pulled Chicken Barbecue • Chicken and Shrimp Gumbo

Roast Turkey with Pan Gravy

Baked Ham with Ginger-Mustard Glaze

Stuffed Pork Tenderloins • Spaghetti and Meatballs

Prime Rib with Roasted Potatoes

Beef Tenderloin with Madeira Sauce

Baked Lasagna • Big Meat Chili

Ropa Vieja with Yellow Rice

Beef Burgundy • Pastitsio

Braised Lamb Shanks with Vegetables

Herbed Leg of Lamb with Pan-Roasted Potatoes

Big-Crowd Vegetarian Chili

Chili is a natural for feeding a big crowd, and a hearty meatless version will please not only vegetarians, but also the many people who are simply trying to cut back on red meat. This is a particularly tasty dish, with smoky heat from chipotle chiles, and a sauce thickened and smoothed with masa harina, which is available wherever Mexican foods are sold. If you can't find it, omit it and the final cup of water. Because the beans are canned, the chili takes less than an hour to whip together.

¼ cup extra-virgin olive oil

2 onions, diced

1 red bell pepper, diced

1 green bell pepper, diced

2 jalapeños, seeded and diced

6 garlic cloves, chopped

2 tablespoons chili powder, or more to taste

2–3 teaspoons ground chipotle chile, or 1 canned chipotle chile in adobo sauce, minced, or more to taste

2 teaspoons dried oregano, or more to taste

1½ teaspoons ground cumin, or more to taste

6 (15-ounce) cans pinto beans, rinsed and drained

1 (16-ounce) can unseasoned tomato sauce

1 (15-ounce) can diced tomatoes with juice

1 (6-ounce) can tomato paste

5 cups water

Salt and freshly ground black pepper

½ cup masa harina

Chopped fresh cilantro, to serve

Sour cream, to serve

Grated Monterey Jack cheese, to serve

Tortilla chips or saltine crackers, to serve

1. Heat the oil in large heavy saucepan or Dutch oven over medium-high heat. Add the onions, bell peppers, jalapeño, and garlic and sauté until the onions soften, about 5 minutes.

2. Stir in the chili powders, oregano, and cumin. Mix in the beans, tomato sauce, diced tomatoes, tomato paste, and 4 cups of the water. Bring the chili to a boil, stirring occasionally. Reduce the heat the heat to medium-low and simmer until the flavors blend, stirring occasionally to prevent scorching, about 30 minutes. Season to taste with salt and pepper.

3. Stir together the masa harina and remaining 1 cup water. Stir into the chili. Bring to a boil, stirring occasionally, until the chili thickens. Taste and adjust the seasoning.

4. Ladle the chili into bowls. Pass the chopped cilantro, sour cream, cheese, and tortilla chips separately.

SERVES 12 TO 16

Stretching Strategy

To stretch a batch of chili for a bigger crowd, serve with taco shells or tortillas and encourage people to use the chili as a filling for tacos or burritos. Serve with chopped lettuce, chopped tomatoes, sliced olives, and guacamole (page 11), as well as the usual grated cheese, sour cream, and cilantro. Serving the chili as a taco or burrito filling is also a good way to use up leftovers.

Pizza Party Pizzas

For casual entertaining, nothing beats a pizza party. Depending on how relaxed you feel with an audience in the kitchen, you can start baking the pizzas once the guests have arrived — or begin baking before the crowd comes and serve the pizzas warm from the oven. Make one pizza plain for the picky eaters, and go wild with the toppings on the others. A green salad completes the meal.

Dough

About 8 cups unbleached all-purpose flour

2 tablespoons salt

3 cups warm (110° to 115°F) water

2 (¼-ounce) packets or 2 tablespoons active dry yeast

6 tablespoons olive oil

Topping

About 6 cups well-seasoned tomato sauce

8 cups grated mozzarella cheese, (about 2 pounds)

Plus any of these ingredients alone or in combinations that appeal to you: sliced onions, bell peppers, olives, mushrooms, pepperoni; minced garlic; chopped fresh basil; grilled zucchini or eggplant; canned pineapple, anchovies, or clams; cooked and crumbled bacon or sausage

1. Make the pizza dough in two batches. In a food processor fitted with a dough hook or in a large bowl, combine 3¾ cups of the flour and 1 tablespoon of the salt. Measure 1½ cups warm water into a glass measure, add one packet of the yeast, and stir until foamy. Stir in 3 tablespoons of the olive oil.

2. With the motor running, pour the water mixture into the food processor and process until the dough forms a ball. Continue processing for 1 minute, to knead the dough. Turn onto a lightly floured surface and knead until the

dough is springy and elastic, about 2 minutes. The dough should be firm and just slightly sticky — not dry.

3. Place the dough ball in an oiled bowl, turning the dough to coat it with the oil. Cover and let rise until doubled in bulk, about 1 hour. Repeat steps 1, 2, and 3 with the remaining flour, salt, water, yeast, and oil to make a second ball of dough.

4. Preheat the oven to 500°F. Allow extra time to get the oven fully preheated.

5. Place one batch of dough in the refrigerator to retard any further rising. Divide the other batch into two balls. Brush two large baking sheets or pizza pans with oil. Stretch the dough to fit each pan. The dough is now ready for topping.

6. Cover each pizza with about 1½ cups of the tomato sauce, leaving a ½-inch border around the edges. Sprinkle the cheese over the sauce. Scatter a handful of toppings over the cheese, if desired.

7. Bake the pizzas for 12 to 15 minutes, until the crust is crisp and the cheese is melted.

8. When the second pizza goes in the oven, remove the remaining dough from the refrigerator. Repeat steps 5, 6, and 7 to make two more pizzas.

FOUR 10- TO 12-INCH ROUND, OR FOUR 12- BY 15-INCH RECTANGULAR PIZZAS

Crowd-Pleasing Variations

If you like, make a white pizza with goat cheese and vegetables, omitting the sauce and mozzarella. Also, pesto can replace the sauce on one of the pizzas. Variety is the spice of life — and leftover pizza is delicious the next day.

Spaghetti with Three Sauces

Everyone likes spaghetti, right? It's the perfect dish to serve when there will be fussy eaters (kids) in the crowd. You can make it more interesting by serving a few different sauces — all of them made in advance. Everyone gets the sauce of their choice; you don't have to feel like you are having a dinner party of "nursery food;" and the fussiest eater can eat his noodles with just plain butter. Add Italian bread and salad for an easy dinner.

Pesto Sauce

- 1½ cups tightly packed fresh basil leaves
- 2 garlic cloves
- 3 tablespoons toasted pine nuts, almonds, or walnuts
- ¼ cup extra-virgin olive oil, plus additional oil for sealing the top, if needed
- 3 tablespoons freshly grated Parmesan cheese

  Salt and freshly ground black pepper

Marinara Sauce

- ¼ cup extra-virgin olive oil
- 1 onion, halved and sliced
- 4 garlic cloves, minced
- 1 (28-ounce) can tomato purée
- 1 (28-ounce) can diced tomatoes
- ¼ cup chopped fresh basil leaves
- 1 tablespoon dried oregano
- 1 teaspoon mixed Italian herbs
- ½ teaspoon sugar, or to taste

  Salt and freshly ground black pepper

Creamy Mushroom Sauce

- 2 cups chicken broth
- 1½ cups whipping cream
- 4 large garlic cloves
- ¼ teaspoon crushed red pepper flakes
- 1 cup freshly grated Parmesan cheese
- 3 tablespoons butter
- 1 pound cremini or button mushrooms, sliced
- 2 leeks, trimmed and sliced

To Serve

- 2 pounds pasta

  Freshly grated Parmesan cheese

1. To make the pesto, combine the basil, garlic, and pine nuts in a food processor fitted with a metal blade. Process until finely chopped. Add the oil through the feed tube with the motor running and continue processing until you have a paste. Briefly mix in the cheese, and salt and pepper to taste. Set aside for at least 20 minutes to allow the flavors to develop, if you are going to use it immediately. Otherwise, spoon the pesto into an airtight container and pour in enough oil to cover surface completely and exclude any air. Seal and store in the refrigerator for up to 1 week, or in the freezer for up to 6 months.

2. To make the marinara sauce, heat the oil in a large saucepan over medium-high heat. Add the onion and garlic and sauté until softened, about 3 minutes. Add the tomato purée, diced tomatoes, basil, oregano, and Italian herbs. Bring to a boil, reduce the heat, and simmer for 30 minutes, stirring occasionally. Add the sugar, and salt and pepper to taste. Keep warm.

3. To make the mushroom sauce, combine the broth, cream, garlic, and crushed red pepper in a medium saucepan. Bring to a boil. Reduce the heat and simmer until liquid is reduced by about one-third, about 20 minutes. Remove from the heat. Mix in the cheese. Cover and keep warm.

4. Melt the butter in large nonstick skillet over medium-high heat. Add mushrooms and leeks and sauté until the mushrooms and leeks are tender, about 10 minutes. Stir the mushrooms and leeks into the cream sauce. Keep warm.

5. Bring a large pot of salted water to a boil. Add the pasta and cook until al dente. Remove about 1 cup of the cooking water for thinning the pesto. Drain well.

6. Divide the pasta among three large serving bowls. Top each bowl with one kind of sauce and toss, reserving one-third of each sauce for serving. Adjust the pesto pasta with reserved pasta cooking water, as needed. Serve immediately, passing additional Parmesan (and sauce) at the table.

SERVES 8

Pesto Spinach Lasagna

The trick with any vegetarian lasagna is to "beef" up the flavor and avoid a watery mush. This recipe, with its mixture of pesto and spinach, does the trick.

1 (10-ounce) package frozen chopped spinach, thawed, and squeezed dry

1 pound ricotta cheese

1½ cups prepared pesto (homemade or a store-bought 12-ounce container)

1 cup shredded Parmesan cheese

Salt and freshly ground black pepper

1 large egg, lightly beaten

5 cups homemade or commercially prepared spaghetti sauce

12 no-boil lasagna noodles

3 cups grated mozzarella cheese (about 12 ounces)

1. Preheat the oven to 350°F. Oil a 9- by 13-inch baking dish.

2. Combine the spinach, ricotta, pesto, and Parmesan in medium bowl. Season to taste with salt and pepper; stir in the egg.

3. Spread 1 cup of the sauce in the prepared dish. Arrange three noodles side by side on top of the sauce. Spread one-third of the spinach mixture over the noodles, then one-quarter of the mozzarella. Repeat the layering with the sauce, noodles, spinach mixture, and mozzarella two more times. Top with the remaining three noodles, sauce, and grated cheese. Cover the lasagna with foil.

4. Bake the lasagna for 35 minutes. Uncover and bake until the lasagna is heated through and the cheese on top is melted, about 20 minutes longer.

5. Let stand for 10 minutes before serving.

SERVES 6 TO 8

Cooking Large Amounts of Pasta

Spaghetti suppers can be real crowd-pleasers. Different people can make different sauces, or several tomato sauces can be combined to make one rich-tasting sauce. The tricky part is the pasta. Here are some cooking tips:

- Cook the pasta just until al dente, especially if you will be reheating later.
- Use a tall, lightweight pot with a lid.
- Allow 5 quarts of water and 1 tablespoon salt for each pound of pasta.
- You can reuse the pasta-cooking water once. After that, it becomes too starchy to cook properly.
- Add pasta only when the water comes to a rolling boil. Lower long pasta into the water gradually as it bends. Pour short pasta into boiling water in a steady stream. Stir gently and occasionally to prevent sticking.
- Cover the pot to cook the top pasta at the same rate as the bottom.
- Start timing when the water returns to a rolling boil.
- Begin checking for doneness 2 minutes before you expect it to be done.

- Serve at once, or toss the pasta with sauce or butter to prevent it from sticking to itself. Stir to cool; avoid rinsing in cold water unless you are going to use it for pasta salad. Rinsing the pasta makes the entire dish watery and keeps the sauce from sticking to the pasta.
- What about making pasta in advance and reheating just before serving? If can be done. Cook the pasta until just barely done. Drain and rinse it with icy cold water until it is completely cold, and drain again. When drained, mix in a light olive oil. Store in the refrigerator in an airtight container. Reheat a few servings at a time by dipping the pasta in boiling water. Keep fresh boiling water on hand and replace the water when it becomes cloudy. Bring the pasta to a hot temperature, drain, and serve.

Big-Crowd Vegetarian Pasta Casserole

When organizing a potluck for a big crowd, it is a good idea to provide a couple of substantial main dishes, such as this vegetarian pasta casserole. It is less fuss to make than lasagna, but just as welcome.

2 pounds small pasta shells	1 (14-ounce) can artichoke hearts (about 6 artichoke hearts), rinsed, drained, and quartered
3 tablespoons extra-virgin olive oil	2 (26-ounce) jars spaghetti sauce
1 onion, diced	1 (28-ounce) can diced tomatoes with juice
2 green bell peppers, diced	Salt and freshly ground pepper
2 red bell peppers, diced	4 cups grated mozzarella cheese (about 1 pound)
2 medium-sized zucchini, quartered lengthwise and sliced	2 cups grated Parmesan cheese
4 garlic cloves, minced	
1 pound mushrooms, trimmed and sliced	

1. Cook the pasta in at least 10 quarts of boiling salted water until just done. Drain well. Transfer to a large mixing bowl.

2. Preheat the oven to 350°F.

3. Heat 2 tablespoons of the oil in a large skillet over medium-high heat. Add the onion, bell peppers, zucchini, and garlic and sauté until the vegetables are limp, about 6 minutes. Use a slotted spoon to transfer the vegetables to the bowl with the pasta.

4. Return the skillet to medium-high heat. Add another 1 tablespoon oil to the skillet. Add the mushrooms and sauté until well browned, about 8 minutes.

Scrape the mushrooms and their juices into the bowl with the pasta and vegetables. Add the artichokes.

5. Add the spaghetti sauce and tomatoes to the pasta and mix well. Season to taste with salt and pepper. Mix in half the mozzarella and half the Parmesan. Transfer the mixture to a large roasting pan. Sprinkle the remaining cheeses on top.

6. Bake for 1 hour. Serve hot.

SERVES 12 TO 16

Advance Preparations

The casserole can be assembled up to 3 days in advance, refrigerated, then baked on the day of the party. Allow at least 30 minutes additional baking time if the casserole goes into the oven directly from the refrigerator.

You will need a roasting pan large enough to hold a 25-pound turkey. Do yourself a favor and bake the casserole in a disposable foil pan to save on cleanup after the party.

Orzo with Shrimp, Spinach, and Artichokes

This luxurious company dinner can be assembled in no time at all. The most time-consuming chore is simply peeling the shrimp. A tossed salad and crusty French or Italian bread completes the meal.

1 pound orzo (rice-shaped pasta)

1 (1-pound) bag frozen spinach

2 tablespoons extra-virgin olive oil

2 shallots, minced

1 (15-ounce) can diced tomatoes in juice

½ cup dry white wine

½ teaspoon crushed red pepper flakes

Salt and freshly ground black pepper

1½ pounds uncooked medium shrimp, peeled and deveined

1 (14-ounce) can artichoke hearts (about 6 artichoke hearts), rinsed, drained, and quartered

2 tablespoons chopped fresh basil

2 garlic cloves, chopped

8 ounces feta cheese, crumbled, (about 1½ cups)

1. Cook the orzo in plenty of boiling salted water until just done. Add the spinach to the pot with the orzo, then drain. (This brief contact with the boiling water will defrost the spinach.) Drain well and return to the pot in which it cooked.

2. Preheat the oven to 400°F. Lightly brush a 9- by 13-inch glass baking dish with oil. Transfer the orzo and spinach to the baking dish.

3. Heat the oil in a large skillet over medium-high heat. Add the shallot and sauté until limp, about 2 minutes. Add the tomatoes with juice, wine, and crushed red pepper. Simmer, uncovered, until the sauce is somewhat reduced, stirring occasionally, about 3 minutes. Season the sauce with salt and pepper.

4. Add the tomato sauce to the orzo mixture, along with the shrimp, artichokes, basil, garlic, and half the feta. Mix well and transfer to the prepared baking dish. Top with the remaining feta.

5. Bake the casserole until heated through, about 30 minutes. Serve hot.

SERVES 6 TO 8

Crowd-Pleasing Variations

- Allergic to seafood? Substitute 3 cups of cooked chicken for the shrimp.

- You can assemble the casserole in advance and hold it in the refrigerator for a few hours. Add 10 to 15 minutes to the baking time.

Big-Crowd Pasta Casserole with Sausage

Lasagna is almost a cliché at large potlucks. Defy expectations by providing a pasta casserole instead — less work for you and easier to serve. Italian turkey sausage is lower in fat than pork sausage and will be appreciated by your health-conscious guests.

2 pounds rotini or other corkscrew-shaped pasta

3 tablespoons extra-virgin olive oil

2 onions, halved and thinly sliced

3 green bell peppers, julienned

3 red bell peppers, julienned

4 garlic cloves, minced

2 pounds hot or sweet Italian sausage (turkey or pork) removed from its casings

2 (26-ounce) jars spaghetti sauce

1 (28-ounce) can diced tomatoes with juice

Salt and freshly ground pepper to taste

4 cups grated mozzarella cheese (about 1 pound)

2 cups grated Parmesan cheese

1. Cook the pasta in at least 10 quarts of boiling salted water until just done. Drain well. Transfer to a large mixing bowl.

2. Preheat the oven to 350°F.

3. Heat 2 tablespoons of the oil in a large skillet over medium-high heat. Add the onions, bell peppers, and garlic and sauté until the vegetables are limp, about 6 minutes. Use a slotted spoon to transfer the vegetables to the bowl with the pasta.

4. Return the skillet to medium-high heat. Add another tablespoon oil to the skillet. Add the sausage and sauté until well browned, about 8 minutes, breaking up the sausage as it cooks. Use a slotted spoon to transfer the sausage into the bowl with the pasta and vegetables.

5. Add the spaghetti sauce and tomatoes to the pasta and mix well. Season to taste with salt and pepper. Mix in half the mozzarella and half the Parmesan cheeses. Transfer the mixture to a large roasting dish. Sprinkle the remaining cheeses on top.

6. Bake for 1 hour. Serve hot.

SERVES 12 TO 16

Strange to see how a good dinner and feasting reconciles everybody.

—SAMUEL PEPYS

Lemon-Garlic Roast Chicken Breasts

Chicken breasts work very well for serving a crowd — simple to prepare, easy to serve, and minus the mess of carving a whole chicken. When roasting a whole chicken, the breast meat sometimes dries out while you are waiting for the dark meat to cook through. With this recipe, the white meat, cooked on the bone, stays moist and tender. Even those who prefer dark meat will love these juicy, flavorful roasted chicken breasts.

6   garlic cloves

Zest and juice of 1 medium lemon

1   tablespoon fresh rosemary

1   tablespoon fresh parsley (leaves only)

6   tablespoons extra-virgin olive oil

Salt and freshly ground black pepper

6   chicken breast halves with skin and bones

1   cup chicken broth

1   tablespoon butter, cut into small pieces

1. Combine the garlic, lemon zest and juice, rosemary, and parsley in a blender and process until finely chopped. With the motor running, add 4 tablespoons of the olive oil and process until well incorporated. Season to taste with salt and pepper.

2. Pour the marinade over the chicken breasts in a baking dish or resealable plastic bag. Move the breasts around to completely coat with the marinade. Marinate in the refrigerator for 3 to 8 hours.

3. Preheat the oven to 500°F. Set out a roasting pan big enough to hold the chicken in a single layer.

4. Heat the remaining 2 tablespoons olive oil in a large skillet over high heat. Remove the chicken from the marinade and place skin side down in the

skillet in a single layer (you may have to do this step in two batches). Brown the chicken on the first side for 5 to 6 minutes. Make sure the skin is well-browned, as this will be the only browning step. Turn and brown the second side, 4 to 6 minutes. Transfer the chicken skin side up to the roasting pan. Set the skillet aside.

5. Roast the chicken for about 15 minutes, until the juices run clear and the flesh is white throughout.

6. Meanwhile, deglaze the skillet by returning to high heat and adding the chicken broth, stirring to bring up all the browned bits. Boil over high heat until the broth reduces by half, about 4 minutes. Whisk in the butter, piece by piece, whisking until it is fully incorporated before adding the next piece. Keep warm.

7. When the chicken is done, transfer to a serving platter and keep warm. Pour any pan juices into the sauce in the skillet and boil for 1 minute. Spoon the sauce over the chicken and serve.

SERVES 6

Stretching Strategy

The recipe is easily multiplied. If serving at a potluck or buffet, cut the breasts horizontally in half to make smaller pieces; a pair of poultry shears does the best job of cutting through the bones.

Braised Chicken Provençale

This is a very rich chicken dish. One thigh will be enough for most guests, but some people may want more, so be sure to figure on a few extra servings. The chicken, with its rich tomato sauce and vegetables, is terrific served over egg noodles. A green salad completes the meal.

12 bone-in chicken thighs

1 cup unbleached all-purpose flour

Salt and freshly ground black pepper

2 tablespoons fresh thyme leaves, or 2 teaspoons dried

2 to 3 tablespoons extra-virgin olive oil

2 leeks or 1 onion, halved and thinly sliced

1 red or green bell pepper, thinly sliced

2 fennel bulbs, trimmed and thinly sliced

1 (28-ounce) can diced tomatoes with juice

1 cup red wine

6 garlic cloves, minced

4 bay leaves

1 cup Niçoise olives, pitted

Chopped fresh parsley, to serve

1. Preheat the oven to 300°F.

2. Remove any fat from the chicken, rinse, and pat dry. Place the flour in a shallow bowl. Season with salt, pepper, and 1 tablespoon of the thyme. Dredge the chicken in the flour, shaking off any excess.

3. Heat 2 tablespoons of the oil in a large skillet over medium-high heat. Add a single layer of the chicken and brown, turning as needed, about 3 minutes per side. Adjust the temperature as needed to allow the chicken to brown but not scorch. (Make sure the chicken is well browned or the final dish will look anemic.) Remove the browned chicken to a large roasting pan and keep warm. Repeat until all the chicken is browned.

4. Heat the remaining 1 tablespoon oil in the skillet, if needed. Add the leeks, bell pepper, and fennel and sauté until softened, about 3 minutes.

5. Spoon the sautéed vegetables over the chicken in the roasting pan. Add the tomatoes, wine, garlic, remaining 1 tablespoon fresh thyme, bay leaves, and olives.

6. Cover and bake until the chicken is cooked through, about 1½ hours.

7. With a slotted spoon, transfer the chicken to a large platter and keep warm. Taste and adjust seasonings in the sauce. Remove the bay leaves. Pour the sauce and vegetables over the chicken on the serving platter. Serve immediately, garnished with parsley.

SERVES 6 TO 12

A Fresh Take on Leftovers

This is a very easy dish to prepare, and practically foolproof. Leftovers are easily frozen. You can even take the leftover chicken, remove it from the bone, chop into bite-size pieces, and combine it with the vegetables, sauce, and enough chicken broth to make a hearty, delicious soup that tastes as if it simmered on the back burner all day.

Pulled Chicken Barbecue

When it comes to casual entertaining, it doesn't get much better than this. The chicken is slowly baked in a homemade barbecue sauce until it is fork tender and deeply infused with barbecue flavor. While the chicken bakes, you are free to be busy elsewhere. Serve with sandwich buns, coleslaw, pickles, potato chips, and plenty of napkins. Cold beer and lemonade would not go amiss.

8 chicken leg quarters, skins removed (7 to 8 pounds)	1 tablespoon soy sauce
1 onion, diced	1 tablespoon chili powder
2 garlic cloves, minced	2 teaspoons salt
1½ cups ketchup	1 to 2 teaspoons ground chipotle chile powder, or ½ to 1 chipotle chile in adobo sauce, minced
⅓ cup cider vinegar	½ teaspoon black pepper
⅓ cup packed light or dark brown sugar	12 buns
2 tablespoons Worcestershire sauce	

1. Preheat the oven to 300°F.

2. Arrange the chicken leg quarters in a single layer in a large roasting pan. Scatter the onion and garlic on top.

3. Combine the ketchup, vinegar, brown sugar, Worcestershire sauce, soy sauce, chili powder, salt, chipotle, and black pepper in a medium bowl. Stir until well blended. Pour over the chicken. Cover the roasting pan with foil.

4. Bake for about 3 hours, until the chicken is fork tender and pulls apart easily. Remove from the oven and let cool slightly.

5. When the chicken is cool enough to handle, pull the chicken off the bones into small chunks and transfer to a saucepan. Pour the cooking sauce into a tall

container to allow the fat to rise to the surface. Skim off the fat and pour the liquid over the chicken.

6. Reheat the chicken, stirring frequently. The chicken will break apart into shreds.

7. Serve hot, spooned over the buns.

SERVES 8 TO 10

BARBECUE SMOKE   The chipotle chile is necessary for adding a smoked flavor (chipotles are smoked, dried jalapeños). You can buy it ground as a powder or in a can in adobo sauce. If you can't find chipotles in one form or another, substitute a teaspoon of liquid smoke.

Advance Preparations

This dish is perfect for making ahead. The chicken can be reheated later in the day, or even the next day. It also freezes well, though you may need to moisten the chicken with additional barbecue sauce (use your favorite bottled sauce). The recipe can be multiplied easily, even if the chicken won't fit in a single layer in the roasting pan; increase the baking time if cooking a larger quantity.

Chicken leg quarters are the least expensive chicken parts you can buy, which makes them easy on the budget. But if you don't mind paying a little more, buying 8 pounds of skinless chicken thighs will eliminate the step of having to remove the skins and makes the job of removing the meat from the bone much simpler.

Chicken and Shrimp Gumbo

To make things easy on yourself, consider this a two-day job. Cook the chicken and stock on one day and finish the job on the second day. Gumbo ingredients can be varied according to what you have on hand, but it must include the Cajun flavor trinity of onion, peppers, and celery, and it should be thickened either with okra or a darkened roux or both.

Chicken and Stock

3 to 4 pounds chicken parts

2 onions, chopped

3 celery stalks, chopped

1 bunch parsley

Water to cover (about 12 cups)

Gumbo

1 tablespoon extra-virgin olive oil

1 onion, diced

1 green bell pepper, diced

2 celery stalks, thinly sliced

4 garlic cloves, minced

1 pound fresh or frozen okra, stems removed and pods sliced (about 4 cups) (optional)

½ pound andouille or other spicy smoked sausage, sliced or diced

1½ cups diced tomatoes with juice (fresh or canned)

¼ cup chopped fresh parsley

2 bay leaves

2 tablespoons fresh thyme leaves

½ teaspoon black pepper, or to taste

½ teaspoon white pepper, or to taste

½ teaspoon cayenne, or to taste

Salt

⅔ cup canola or other vegetable oil

⅔ cup unbleached all-purpose flour

1 pound medium shrimp, peeled and deveined

½ cup chopped scallions

4 to 6 cups cooked white rice, to serve

Filé powder, to serve

Louisiana-style hot sauce, such as Frank's or Crystal, to serve

1. To make the chicken and stock, combine the chicken, onion, celery, and parsley in a large soup pot. Cover with cold water. Bring just to a boil. Immediately reduce the heat and simmer gently for 2 hours with the lid partially on. Strain and discard the vegetables. Remove the meat from the bones and set aside. Discard the skin and bones. Chill the stock for several hours. Skim off the fat that rises to the top and hardens.

2. To make the gumbo, heat the olive oil in a large soup pot. Add the onion, green pepper, celery, and garlic, and sauté until the onion is limp, about 4 minutes.

3. Add 8 cups of the defatted broth, okra, if using, sausage, tomatoes, parsley, bay leaves, thyme, black and white peppers, cayenne, and salt to taste. Bring to a boil, then simmer for about 30 minutes.

4. Meanwhile, in a large skillet, combine the canola oil and flour, stirring until you have a smooth paste. Cook over medium heat until the paste is a rich brown, 10 to 20 minutes. Do not let the mixture burn.

5. Carefully stir the roux into the gumbo, protecting your arms from hot spatters. Add the reserved chicken, shrimp, and scallions. Taste and adjust the seasonings. Simmer for another 15 minutes. Remove the bay leaves.

6. To serve, ladle the gumbo over rice in large soup bowls. Pass the filé powder and hot sauce at the table.

SERVES 8 TO 12

THE FLAVORS OF GUMBO   The okra is optional, but recommended. It will stretch the soup further, but it can be difficult to find. Filé powder is found in the spice section of most supermarkets. It is made from the dried leaves of the sassafras tree and is traditionally used to thicken and flavor gumbo. If you can't find it, just omit it.

Roast Turkey with Pan Gravy

Fresh, locally raised turkeys, ones that are not processed, basted, or in any other way made unnatural, are so superior to supermarket birds that there is no comparison. Fresh birds are juicier and tastier. So the best way to cook a delicious turkey is to start with a fresh one. The rest is easy. It generally takes 15 minutes per pound to roast an unstuffed bird, so do the math before you begin.

1 turkey, about 20 pounds

Salt and freshly ground black pepper

Poultry seasoning

Paprika

3 onions: 2 quartered and 1 chopped

3 celery stalks, quartered

Butter

Water

6 cups chicken broth

Stems from 1 bunch parsley

¾ cup all-purpose unbleached flour

1. Preheat the oven to 350°F with the oven rack in its lowest position.

2. Remove the giblets and neck from turkey; reserve for making the gravy. Rinse the turkey with cold running water, drain well, and pat dry.

3. Sprinkle the turkey inside and out with salt. Sprinkle with pepper, poultry seasoning, and paprika. Stuff the body cavity with 1 quartered onion and 1 stalk of celery. Depending on how the turkey was prepared, tie the legs and tail together with string, push the drumsticks under the band of skin, or use the stuffing clamp to secure the legs.

4. Place the turkey, breast side up, on rack in a large roasting pan. Brush the turkey with butter. Scatter the chopped onion in the pan and pour in ½ cup water. Cover the breast loosely with aluminum foil. Roast, basting with water or pan drippings every 30 minutes, until an instant-read thermometer

plunged into the deepest part of the thigh registers 165° to 170°F. This should take about 15 minutes per pound. About 1 hour before the bird should be done, remove the foil.

5. While the turkey is roasting, make a broth. Combine the giblets and neck in a medium saucepan with 6 cups of the chicken broth, the remaining onion, the remaining celery, and the parsley stems. Bring to a boil, reduce the heat, and simmer for 1 hour. Strain out the solids and refrigerate the broth until needed for the gravy.

6. When the turkey is done, place on warm large platter; keep warm. Let the turkey stand for at least 20 minutes before carving. While the turkey is resting, prepare the gravy.

7. To make the gravy, pour the pan drippings through a sieve into 2-quart measuring cup or medium bowl. Add 1 cup of the giblet broth to the roasting pan and stir until the brown bits are loosened. Pour into the drippings in the measuring cup. Add enough broth to measure 6 cups. Let stand a few minutes until the fat separates from meat juice. Discard the fat or reserve for the gravy.

8. Heat ¾ cup turkey fat or butter in a medium saucepan over medium heat. Stir in the flour and cook until smooth and golden brown. Gradually stir in the pan drippings mixture and cook, stirring, until the gravy boils and thickens slightly. Taste and adjust the seasoning.

9. Carve the turkey. Pour the gravy into a gravy boat and serve with the turkey.

SERVES 15 TO 20

HOW MUCH TURKEY? When making your purchases, generally allow 1 pound of turkey per person. And don't forget to allow plenty of time in the refrigerator for thawing a frozen turkey (another good reason to buy fresh).

Elements of a Successful Potluck

Balanced Offerings

I've observed a trend at potlucks recently: an abundance of salads and desserts. The salads, which are usually dressed at the party, are quick to throw together and are easy to transport. The desserts may be made ahead and are also easy to transport. That leaves the table bereft of enough hearty main dishes and hot vegetable dishes. As a host or hostess, you may want to compensate for this yourself. As a guest, know that anyone who brings a hearty hot entrée or vegetable side dish will be especially appreciated.

Quick Cleanup

Many potluck offerings can be prepared in disposable foil pans. These pans make very quick work of the post-party cleanup, and save you the trouble of locating your kitchen belongings before leaving the gathering. If your dish feels very heavy in the disposable pan, transport the whole thing on a sturdy baking sheet.

Glazes or marinades containing sugar (as in the Baked Ham opposite) can make a terrible mess when baking. If you choose to use real roasting pans, a layer of aluminum foil lining the bottom of the pan can save a lot of scrubbing effort. Do not use foil linings with tomato sauce-based dishes; the acid in the tomatoes reacts with the aluminum and can adversely affect the taste of the dish.

Baked Ham with Ginger-Mustard Glaze

A ham is a fully cooked piece of meat. All you do is heat and glaze it, so the quality of the ham makes all the difference. If presentation is the most important thing, buy a boneless, spiral-cut ham, but bone-in hams are generally juicier and will leave you with a lovely bone for making soup.

- ¾ cup whole-grain Dijon mustard
- ¼ cup packed light or dark brown sugar
- 1 tablespoon minced garlic
- 2 tablespoons ginger preserves (available where British foods are sold)
- 1 teaspoon finely ground black pepper
- 1 (11- to 13-pound) fully cooked bone-in ham (shank or butt end)

1. Preheat the oven to 400°F. Line a large roasting pan with a layer of aluminum foil or use a disposable aluminum pan.

2. Trim any tough rind and fat from upper side of ham, leaving a ¼-inch-thick layer of fat. Using a long sharp knife, score the fat in a 1-inch-wide diamond pattern. Place the ham in the prepared pan. Bake the ham until heated through, about 10 minutes per pound.

3. Meanwhile, mix the mustard, brown sugar, garlic, preserves, and pepper in a medium bowl.

4. About 30 minutes before the ham will be fully heated, remove the pan from the oven. Spread the mustard mixture generously over top and sides of ham. Return to oven and continue to bake until mustard coating is golden brown, about 30 minutes.

5. Transfer the ham to a platter. Slice into ½-inch-thick slices and serve.

SERVES 12

Stuffed Pork Tenderloins

This elegant main course is perfect for a dinner party. The pork is deliciously tender and flavorful, and the presentation is impressive. Pork tenderloins are often packaged in pairs, so make sure you aren't buying more than you need.

Pork

- 2 (¾- to 1¼-pound) pork tenderloins, trimmed of silverskin and fat
- 6 tablespoons butter
- 4 scallions, white and tender green parts, thinly sliced
- 1 celery stalk, finely diced
- 4 garlic cloves, minced
- 4 cups fresh bread crumbs
- 1 tablespoon chopped fresh rosemary, or 1 teaspoon dried
- 1 tablespoon chopped fresh thyme, or 1 teaspoon dried

Salt and freshly ground black pepper
- 1 tablespoon Dijon mustard
- 2 tablespoons extra-virgin olive oil

Pan Sauce

- 2 cups chicken broth
- ¼ cup dry white wine or sherry
- ¼ cup minced shallots (1 to 3 shallots)

Salt and fresh ground black pepper
- 1 tablespoon butter

HOMEMADE BREAD CRUMBS Fresh bread crumbs are easily made processing sandwich bread in a food processor. Six slices of packaged white or whole wheat bread will make about 4 cups.

1. Butterfly the tenderloins: Slice the length of each tenderloin, so that it opens like a book with an even ¼-inch to ½-inch thickness; do not slice all the way through. Pound the tenderloin even thinner between two sheets of plastic wrap using a meat pounder or the flat bottom of a small, heavy skillet.

2. Place a roasting pan in the oven and preheat the oven to 400°F.

3. Melt the butter in a large skillet over medium-high heat. Add the scallions, celery, and garlic, and sauté until the vegetables are limp, about 3 minutes. Stir in the bread crumbs, rosemary, and thyme, and mix until well blended. Season to taste with salt and pepper.

4. Brush the mustard along the inside of the tenderloins. Spread the bread crumb mixture over the mustard. Roll up each roast along its length like a jelly roll and tie with butcher's twine. Brush the outside of the tenderloins with the olive oil and season generously with the salt and pepper.

5. Place the tenderloins in the preheated roasting pan and roast for 20 to 25 minutes — until meat reaches an internal temperature of 145° to 150°F.

6. Remove the meat from the pan and let stand, loosely covered with foil, while you prepare the pan sauce.

7. To make the sauce, place the roasting pan over two burners set on medium-high. Add the broth, wine, and shallots and bring to a boil, stirring to scrape up any browned bits from the bottom of the pan. Continue to boil until the sauce reduces by half and becomes syrupy. Remove from the heat and strain out the solids. Swirl in the butter, a little bit a time. Season with salt and pepper.

8. Remove the butcher's twine, carve the meat into slices about ½-inch thick, and serve with the pan sauce.

SERVES 6

Advance Preparations

The pork can be filled, rolled, and refrigerated earlier in the day and roasted right before you are ready to serve.

Spaghetti and Meatballs

Nine out of ten little kids request mom's spaghetti and meatballs for their birthday suppers. You can easily multiply the sauce and meatballs to serve a bigger crowd. When cooking larger quantities of pasta, remember that for every pound of pasta, you'll need about 5 quarts of water and 1 tablespoon of salt. If you don't have a large enough pot, cook the pasta in two batches.

Sauce

- 2 tablespoons extra-virgin olive oil
- 1 onion, diced
- ½ pound white mushrooms, trimmed and sliced (optional)
- 1 (28-ounce) can tomato purée
- 1 (28-ounce can) diced tomatoes with juice
- 4 garlic cloves, minced
- ¾ cup dry red wine
- ½ cup chicken or beef broth or water
- 4 teaspoons mixed Italian herbs

  Salt and freshly ground black pepper
- ½–1 teaspoon sugar (optional)

Meatballs

- 1 onion, quartered
- ¼ cup loosely packed fresh parsley leaves
- 4 garlic cloves
- 2 slices sandwich bread
- 1 pound Italian pork or turkey sausage, removed from its casings
- ½ pound ground beef
- 2 large eggs

  Salt and freshly ground black pepper
- 2 tablespoons extra-virgin olive oil

To Assemble

1–1¼ pounds spaghetti

  Freshly grated Parmesan cheese

1. To make the sauce, heat the oil in a large saucepan over medium-high heat. Add the onion and mushrooms and sauté until the mushrooms give up their juice, about 5 minutes. Add the tomato purée, diced tomatoes, garlic, wine, broth, and Italian herbs. Season to taste with salt and pepper. Add sugar if needed to bring the flavors into balance. Bring to a boil, reduce the heat, and simmer, partially covered, while you make the meatballs.

2. To make the meatballs, combine the onion, parsley, and garlic in a food processor and process until finely chopped. Add the bread and process until you have fine crumbs. Add the sausage, beef, eggs, and salt and pepper. Process until well mixed.

3. Heat the oil in a large skillet over medium-high heat. Using two tablespoons, form the meat mixture into meatballs the size of walnuts. Arrange a single layer in the skillet and fry, turning as needed, until browned all over, about 5 minutes. Remove the meatballs with a slotted spoon and add to the simmering sauce. Continue making and browning meatballs until all the meat mixture is used.

4. Simmer the sauce and meatballs, partially covered, for about 1 hour.

5. Bring a large pot of salted water to a boil. Add the spaghetti and cook until al dente. Drain well.

6. Serve the spaghetti topped with the sauce. Pass the Parmesan at the table.

SERVES 6

Prime Rib with Roasted Potatoes

This is the ultimate roast beef — perfect for holidays and special occasions. Figure that each rib serves two people with leftovers, but don't begin with any roast smaller than three ribs. This meat is best served rare and an accurate thermometer is a must — this is too expensive a cut to apply guesswork. For planning purposes, however, figure that if the roast goes in at room temperature, as recommended, you should allow about 15 minutes per pound.

1	(4-rib) prime rib, about 10 pounds, trimmed of excess but not all fat	2	teaspoons coarsely ground black pepper
4	garlic cloves, minced	10	medium-sized potatoes, peeled and halved or quartered
2	tablespoons chopped fresh thyme or rosemary	2	cups beef broth or stock
	Kosher or coarse salt	¼	cup dry red wine

1. Remove the roast from the refrigerator 1 to 2 hours before roasting and allow it to come to room temperature. If the butcher has tied the roast, leave the ties in place. Otherwise, it is not necessary to tie it.

2. Preheat the oven to 450°F.

3. Place the meat, bone side down, in a large roasting pan. Finely chop the garlic and fresh herbs with 1 tablespoon salt and the pepper and rub into the meat.

4. Roast the meat for 20 minutes. Reduce the oven to 350°F and continue to roast for 1 hour.

5. Scatter the potatoes around the meat, turning them in the rendered fat so they are well coated. Return the roasting pan to the oven and roast for about 30 minutes. Check the meat in several places with the instant-read thermometer.

When no spot registers under 120°F for rare, the meat is done. The potatoes should be fork tender on the inside, crispy on the outside. If the potatoes are done before the meat, remove them from the pan and continue roasting the meat until it reaches 120°F in several places. If the meat is done before the potatoes, remove the meat from the roasting pan. Place the meat on a platter under a tent of aluminum foil. Turn the potatoes in the roasting pan, return to the oven, and continue roasting under tender and browned. Transfer to a serving dish and keep warm.

6. Pour off the fat from the roasting pan. Place the roasting pan over two burners on top of the stove. Add the broth and wine. Bring to a boil over high heat and cook, stirring and scraping up any browned bits, until it is reduced by half. Pour into a pitcher or gravy boat to serve.

7. To carve the meat, cut off the butcher's twine, if necessary. If the rib-eye hasn't been completely cut off the bone, tilt the meat onto the side and run your knife parallel to the ribs to separate the meat (the rib-eye) from the rib bones. Slice the now-boneless meat into slices of whatever thickness you prefer and separate the individual ribs by cutting between the bones. Arrange on a serving platter, pouring some of the juices over the meat.

8. Serve the meat and potatoes, passing the *jus* on the side.

SERVES 8

Seated at Life's Dining Table

Roast Beef, Medium, is not only a food. It is a philosophy. Seated at Life's Dining Table, with the menu of Morals before you, your eye wanders a bit over the entrées, the hors d'oeuvres, and the things à la, though you know that Roast Beef, Medium, is safe and sane, and sure.

EDNA FERBER

Beef Tenderloin with Madeira Sauce

With an excellent (and expensive) piece of meat like a tenderloin, a cook's motto should be "First, do no harm." In this case it means, keep the preparation simple and don't overcook! An accurate meat thermometer is helpful and, as with all high-temperature roasting, a good ventilation system is a blessing.

Meat

- 1 (5- to 6-pound) beef tenderloin
- ½ cup loosely packed chopped fresh parsley
- 2 garlic cloves
- 1 tablespoon chopped fresh thyme, or 1 teaspoon dried
- 1 tablespoon chopped fresh rosemary, or 1 teaspoon dried
- 3 tablespoons extra-virgin olive oil
- 1½ teaspoons salt
- ½ teaspoon freshly ground black pepper

Madeira Sauce

- 3 tablespoons butter
- 2 shallots, minced
- ¼ cup all-purpose flour
- ¼ cup Madeira (port or red wine can be substituted)
- 1½ cups beef broth or stock

  Salt and freshly ground black pepper

1. Preheat the oven to 400°F. Lightly oil a large roasting pan.

2. Trim the fat and silverskin from the meat. Either cut off the 6-inch tail and reserve it for a stir-fry, or fold it under. Tie the meat with butcher's twine at 1½-inch intervals to maintain a rounded shape. Combine the parsley, garlic, thyme, rosemary, olive oil, salt, and pepper in a small bowl. Rub all over the meat. Place the meat in the roasting pan.

3. Roast until the thickest part of the roast reads 120°F on an instant-read thermometer for rare, about 40 minutes. If desired, continue roasting to 125° to 130°F for medium rare, or 135° to 140°F for medium.

4. While the meat roasts, make the sauce. Melt the butter in a medium saucepan over medium heat. Add the shallots and sauté until softened, about 3 minutes. Whisk in the flour to make a smooth paste. Add the Madeira and broth, and cook, stirring, until thick, about 5 minutes. Keep warm.

5. Once the meat reaches the desired temperature, remove from the oven and let the meat rest under a tent of aluminum for 15 to 20 minutes. Remove the strings and slice about ½ inch thick.

6. Serve the meat with the sauce.

SERVES 6 TO 8

A SPECIAL OCCASION FAVORITE   A tenderloin is a terrific choice for a holiday or company meal because it is quick and simple to make, easy to carve with virtually no waste, and loved by all.

Baked Lasagna

Lasagna is the first dish people think of when cooking for a crowd. Make yours memorable with a hearty Bolognese meat sauce and béchamel (or white sauce) instead of the ricotta.

Bolognese Sauce

- 3 tablespoons extra-virgin olive oil
- 2 celery stalks, finely chopped
- 1 small onion, finely chopped
- 1 carrot, finely chopped
- 2 garlic cloves, finely chopped
- 1 pound ground beef or pork
  - Salt and freshly ground black pepper
- 1 cup whole milk
- 1 cup dry white wine
- 1 (15-ounce) can diced tomatoes, with juice

Béchamel Sauce

- ¼ cup butter
- ¼ cup unbleached all-purpose flour
- 3 cups whole milk
  - Salt and freshly ground black pepper
  - Pinch freshly grated nutmeg

To Assemble

- 15 no-boil lasagna noodles
- 1 cup freshly grated Parmesan cheese

1. To make the Bolognese sauce, heat the oil in a large saucepan over medium-high heat. Add the celery, onion, carrot, and garlic and sauté until softened, 2 to 3 minutes. Add the beef and season with salt and pepper. Sauté until the meat is no longer pink, 6 to 8 minutes. Add the milk and simmer until evaporated, about 20 minutes. Add the wine and simmer until evaporated, about 20 minutes.

2. Add the tomatoes and simmer for 2 to 3 hours, until the flavors have blended and the sauce is a rich stew, stirring from time to time, to keep the sauce from sticking to the bottom of the pot. Season to taste with salt and pepper.

3. To make the béchamel sauce, melt the butter in a medium saucepan over medium heat. Whisk in the flour to make a smooth paste. Stir in the milk and cook, stirring, until thickened. Season to taste with salt and pepper and nutmeg.

4. Preheat the oven to 350°F. Lightly oil a 9- by 13-inch baking dish.

5. To assemble the lasagna, spread about ¼ cup of the béchamel in the prepared baking dish. Place three lasagna noodles over the sauce. Spread a thin layer of meat sauce over the noodles, then a layer of béchamel, then a sprinkling of Parmesan. Repeat to make five layers. Cover with foil.

6. Bake the lasagna for 30 minutes. Remove the foil and bake for another 10 minutes, until bubbly and browned.

7. Let the lasagna stand for 5 minutes before cutting into serving pieces. Serve warm or hot.

SERVES 6 TO 9

Advance Preparations

The Bolognese sauce is a slow-cooked sauce, but easily made up to 3 days ahead. Let the food processor do the chopping for you. The lasagna can be assembled and held in the refrigerator for a day. Allow extra time for baking if the lasagna goes into the oven cold.

Big Meat Chili

The meat is chopped coarsely in a food processor for this hearty recipe, which gives the chili a more substantial mouth feel. Don't worry about this extra step. If you load your food processor with the meat a pound at a time, it should handle the job in seconds. As long as you have the food processor out, you might as well chop the onions and mince the garlic in the machine, too. You'll find this is faster to make than you might think.

¼ cup extra-virgin olive oil

2 onions, finely chopped

4 garlic cloves, minced

3 pounds boneless beef chuck, coarsely ground in batches in a food processor or by the butcher

¼ cup chili powder

1 tablespoon ground cumin

2 teaspoons dried oregano

1 teaspoon ground chipotle chile, or ½ canned chipotle chile in adobo sauce, minced, or to taste

1 (15-ounce) can unseasoned tomato sauce

1¼ cups beef broth

2 tablespoons red wine vinegar or cider vinegar

1 (19-ounce) can kidney beans, rinsed and drained

1 (4-ounce) can chopped roasted green chiles

Salt and freshly ground black pepper

Grated Cheddar or Monterey Jack cheese, sour cream, tortilla chips, chopped fresh cilantro, to serve

1. Heat the oil in a large saucepan over medium heat. Add the onions and garlic and sauté until softened, 2 to 3 minutes. Add the beef and sauté until browned, 6 to 10 minutes. Add the chili powder, cumin, oregano, and ground chipotle. Cook the mixture, stirring, for 1 minute. Add the tomato sauce, broth, and vinegar. Bring the mixture to a boil. Decrease the heat, cover, and simmer, stirring occasionally, for 60 minutes, until the meat is tender.

2. Add the kidney beans, chiles, and salt and pepper to taste and simmer the mixture, uncovered, for 30 minutes, until the flavors have blended.

3. Set out bowls of grated cheese, sour cream, tortilla chips, and chopped fresh cilantro and serve alongside the hot chili.

SERVES 6 TO 8

Stretching Strategy

Unexpected guests? You can stretch the chili by adding another can of beans and some chopped green or red bell peppers. Or serve it as a taco or burrito filling. Chili can be made several days in advance and will only improve in flavor.

Ropa Vieja with Yellow Rice

Sometimes in the dead of winter, the best dishes to serve evoke the sunny South, as in the Cuban specialty *ropa vieja*, or "old clothes." In this colorful dish, the meat is twice cooked and combined with shreds of colorful bell peppers and onions to make a stew resembling an assortment of colorful rags. Serve with yellow rice to complete the dish.

Beef

- 3 pounds beef flank steak, trimmed
- About 2 quarts water
- 2 onions, quartered
- 2 celery stalks, quartered
- 3 bay leaves
- 1 teaspoon dried oregano
- 1 teaspoon cumin seeds
- 1 teaspoon salt
- ¼ teaspoon whole black peppercorns

Stew

- 3 tablespoons extra-virgin olive oil
- 2 green bell peppers, cut into thin strips
- 2 red bell peppers, cut into thin strips
- 2 yellow or orange bell peppers, cut into thin strips
- 1 onion, halved and thinly sliced
- 3 garlic cloves, minced
- 2 cups braising liquid, plus additional if desired
- 1 (15-ounce) can diced tomatoes with juice
- 3 tablespoons tomato paste
- Salt and freshly ground black pepper
- 2 teaspoons capers
- ½ cup pimiento-stuffed Spanish olives

Yellow Rice

- 3 tablespoons olive oil
- 2 teaspoons cumin seed
- ¼ teaspoon saffron threads
- 2 cups long-grain rice
- 4 cups water
- ¾ teaspoon salt

1. Place the beef in a large pot. Add the water, onions, celery, bay leaves, oregano, cumin, salt, and peppercorns. Simmer, uncovered, for 1½ hours, or until beef is tender.

2. Remove the pot from the heat and cool the meat in the liquid for 30 minutes.

3. Transfer the meat to a platter and cover. Strain the braising liquid into a medium saucepan. Boil until reduced to 3 cups (about half), about 30 minutes.

4. Pull the meat into shreds.

5. Heat the oil in a large Dutch oven over medium-high heat. Add the bell peppers, onion, and garlic and sauté until softened, about 5 minutes. Add the shredded meat, 2 cups of the braising liquid, the tomatoes with juice, and the tomato paste. Season to taste with salt and pepper and simmer, uncovered, for 20 minutes. Add additional braising liquid, if the stew is too dry.

6. While the stew simmers, make the rice. Heat the oil in a medium saucepan over medium heat until hot. Add the cumin seeds and saffron and simmer until the oil is fragrant, about 2 minutes. Stir in the rice and sauté, stirring, for 1 to 2 minutes, until the rice is well coated. Stir in the water and salt and bring to a boil. Cover, reduce the heat, and simmer until the rice is tender and has absorbed all the liquid, about 10 minutes. Remove the pan from the heat and let the rice stand, covered, for 5 minutes. Fluff the rice with a fork.

7. Stir the capers and olives into the stew and simmer, uncovered, for 5 minutes.

8. To serve, spoon the stew over the rice.

SERVES 8

THE TRUE TASTE OF CUBA Replace the saffron with 1 teaspoon of annatto seeds if you can find them. Simmer the oil for about 5 minutes with the annatto and cumin seeds, then strain the oil before proceeding. The flavor is authentic and deliciously floral.

Beef Burgundy

Because the meat is soaked in wine before it is cooked, French *boeuf bourguignon* seems more appropriate for entertaining than everyday beef stew, though the two dishes are similar. Choose an inexpensive cut, such as chuck, bottom round, or short rib, for the beef. A light dry red wine, such as Pinot Noir or Beaujolais, works well as the marinade. Serve the same wine with dinner, along with a good loaf of French bread. The dish is traditionally served with boiled new potatoes or noodles, but mashed potatoes are also a wonderful crowd-pleasing option.

2 pounds boneless beef chuck or bottom round, cut into 2-inch cubes

2 cups red wine

3 tablespoons extra-virgin olive oil

2 garlic cloves, minced

2 bay leaves

Salt and freshly ground black pepper

½ cup unbleached all-purpose flour

4 ounces bacon

1 large onion, very finely diced

2 celery stalks, very finely diced

1 large carrot, very finely diced

1 cup beef broth

2 tablespoons tomato paste

1 tablespoon fresh thyme

1 pound small boiling onions, peeled

8 ounces mushrooms, sliced

¼ cup chopped fresh parsley

1. Combine the meat, wine, olive oil, garlic, and bay leaves in a large bowl. Add 1 teaspoon salt and ½ teaspoon black pepper. Cover and marinate the beef in this mixture in the refrigerator for at least 12 hours and up to 24 hours, turning occasionally.

2. Preheat the oven to 275°F.

3. Drain the meat, reserving the marinade. Toss the meat with the flour in a medium bowl until well coated.

4. Fry the bacon in a large Dutch oven over medium heat until crisp, about 8 minutes. Remove the bacon with a slotted spoon and set aside on paper towels. Drain off all the bacon fat and reserve.

5. Return 2 tablespoons of the bacon fat to the Dutch oven. Add a single layer of beef and brown the beef on all sides, about 6 minutes. Use a slotted spoon to remove the beef from the pan. Repeat until all the beef is browned, adding more bacon fat as needed.

6. Add the onion, celery, and carrot to the Dutch oven, along with more bacon fat if needed, and sauté until softened, about 4 minutes.

7. Add the broth to the Dutch oven and cook, stirring to scrape up any browned bits, for 3 minutes.

8. Stir in the marinade, tomato paste, and thyme. Stir until mixture comes to a boil. Taste and adjust the seasoning. Add the browned beef and cover the Dutch oven.

9. Bake for 2½ to 3 hours, until the beef is tender.

10. Add the boiling onions and mushrooms to the beef and stir well. Continue to bake for 30 minutes, until the onions are tender.

11. Stir well. Sprinkle with the parsley. Serve hot.

SERVES 6

Advance Preparations

If you can, make this dish a day in advance. Overnight, the fat will rise to the surface, making it easy to skim off before reheating the stew.

Pastitsio

Call it Greek lasagna, and you'll have a sense of when you might want to serve pastitsio. It is a great make-ahead dish that is perfect for large gatherings. Although it doesn't seem likely while you are assembling the dish, the noodles set up nicely, making it simple to cut neat squares for serving.

Tomato Sauce

- 2 tablespoons extra-virgin olive oil
- 2 onions, finely chopped
- 1 large eggplant, peeled and cubed
- 1½ pounds ground lamb
- 1 (8-ounce) can unseasoned tomato sauce
- 1 (6-ounce) can tomato paste
- 1 cup water
- 1 teaspoon dried oregano
- ½ teaspoon ground cinnamon
  Salt and freshly ground black pepper
  Sugar

Cream Sauce

- 3 tablespoons butter
- ¼ cup unbleached all-purpose flour
- 3½ cups milk
- 3 eggs, beaten
  Freshly grated nutmeg

To Assemble

- 1 pound rotini or tube-shaped pasta, such as penne
- 1½ cups freshly grated Parmesan cheese

1. Begin heating a large pot of salted water for the pasta.

2. To make the tomato sauce, heat the oil in a large skillet over medium-high heat. Add the onions and eggplant and sauté until the eggplant is lightly colored, about 8 minutes. Add the lamb and sauté until browned, 8 to 10 minutes, crumbling the meat as it cooks.

3. Stir in the tomato sauce, tomato paste, water, oregano, and cinnamon. Season to taste with salt, pepper, and a little sugar. Bring to a boil, then reduce the heat, and simmer until you are ready to assemble the dish.

4. Cook the pasta in the boiling water until just al dente. Drain.

5. To make the cream sauce, melt the butter over medium heat in a small saucepan. Stir in the flour to make a smooth paste. Cook for about 1 minute. Stir in the milk, a little at a time, until all the milk has been added and the sauce is smooth. Cook, stirring constantly until the sauce thickens.

6. Beat the eggs in a small bowl. Add ½ cup of the hot cream sauce, 1 tablespoon at a time, to warm the eggs. Stir the warmed egg mixture into the cream sauce and remove from the heat. Season to taste with salt, pepper, and a grating of fresh nutmeg.

7. Preheat the oven to 350°F. Lightly oil an 11- by 15-inch baking pan.

8. To assemble the casserole, layer half the pasta in the baking pan. Top with half the tomato sauce, then half the Parmesan. Layer the remaining pasta, tomato sauce, and cheese on top. Pour the white sauce over all.

9. Bake, uncovered, for about 40 minutes, or until hot and lightly browned.

10. Let stand for 10 minutes before serving.

SERVES 8 TO 10

Advance Preparations

Like lasagna, pastitsio can be assembled and baked in advance and then reheated. It can even be frozen.

Braised Lamb Shanks with Vegetables

Slow-cooked lamb shanks braised in tomatoes and wine makes a dish to be savored slowly, with red wine and candlelight. Serve with mashed potatoes and French bread for sopping up the gravy. If lamb is too rich for your taste, make this dish with turkey drumsticks instead.

2 tablespoons olive oil (optional)

6 lamb shanks or turkey drumsticks, ¾ to 1 pound each

Salt and freshly ground black pepper

1 large onion, diced

1 (14.5 ounce) can beef or chicken broth (1 ¾ cups)

½ cup white or red wine

1 (28-ounce) can diced tomatoes with juice

1 tablespoon dried thyme

4 garlic cloves, minced

2 bay leaves

1 small rutabaga, peeled and diced

¾ pound baby carrots

1 pound pearl or boiling onions, peeled

1. Preheat the oven to 300°F. Set out a large roasting pan.

2. If making turkey drumsticks, heat the oil in a large skillet over medium-high heat (the lamb will render its own fat). Add the lamb shanks or drumsticks in a single layer and brown on all sides, seasoning with salt and pepper as they cook, about 5 minutes per side. You will have to do this in batches. Transfer the meat to the roasting pan.

3. Add the diced onion to the skillet and sauté until softened, about 3 minutes. Transfer to the roasting pan with a slotted spoon.

4. Pour the broth into the skillet to deglaze all the browned bits. Bring to a boil, stirring. Pour into the roasting pan, along with the wine and tomatoes with their juice. Sprinkle with the thyme, garlic, and bay leaves. Season with salt and pepper. Tightly cover the pan with aluminum foil.

5. Bake for about 1½ hours, until the shanks or drumsticks are tender (a fork inserted into the meaty part will meet with little resistance on its way in or out).

6. Add the rutabaga, carrots, and pearl onions. Replace the cover and continue baking for 1 hour.

7. Remove the bay leaves. Serve hot in large shallow bowls.

SERVES 6

Advance Preparations

This dish is excellent made a day in advance and is easily reheated. An additional advantage of making it ahead is the opportunity it gives you to remove the fat that will rise to the surface of the sauce and congeal. The recipe is easily multiplied if you have a big enough roasting pan. If you like, you can make both lamb shanks and turkey drumsticks in the same pan.

Herbed Leg of Lamb with Pan-Roasted Potatoes

A tender roast of lamb makes a luxurious company dinner, and the pan-roasted potatoes that accompany it are easy to prepare and delicious to enjoy. I recommend buying a boned and tied roast for company; carving a bone-in roast is complicated and potentially messy.

¼	cup fresh rosemary leaves
4	large garlic cloves
3	tablespoons extra-virgin olive oil
	Salt and freshly ground black pepper
1	(5- to 7-pound) boneless leg of lamb
2½	pounds small Yukon Gold or red potatoes, quartered

1. Preheat the oven to 350°F.

2. Combine the rosemary, garlic, 2 tablespoons of the oil, and 1 teaspoon of salt in a food processor and process until the mixture is finely chopped. With tip of a small sharp knife, cut small slits all over the lamb and rub the rosemary mixture over the lamb, rubbing it into the slits. Place the lamb in a large roasting pan.

3. Roast the lamb for 45 minutes.

4. Meanwhile, put the potatoes in a medium saucepan and cover with cold salted water. Bring the water to a boil and cook potatoes, covered, for 5 minutes. Drain the potatoes in a colander and return them to the pot. Toss with the remaining 1 tablespoon of oil. Arrange the potatoes around the lamb and sprinkle with salt and pepper.

5. Continue to roast the lamb with the potatoes, stirring the potatoes occasionally, until a meat thermometer registers 140°F. for medium-rare, 50 to 70 minutes, depending on the size of the roast.

6. Transfer the lamb to a cutting board and let stand 15 minutes. Return the potatoes to the oven, increase the oven temperature to 500°F. and roast the potatoes until golden, 5 to 10 minutes.

7. Carve the lamb, slicing the meat thinly across the grain. Serve with the potatoes.

SERVES 6

A Fresh Take on Leftovers

Turn leftovers into shepherd's pie. Make a gravy by browning a bit of butter and flour together to make a roux, then adding beef broth. Dice the leftover meat and add to the gravy. Add diced onions, diced carrots, frozen peas, frozen corn. Place in a casserole and top with mashed potatoes. This is so much better than the school lunch dish of the same name, made with ground beef.

6 • Grilling Fun

Herbed Garlic Shrimp

Chicken Satay • Simple Grilled Chicken

Grilled Chicken Wings
with Chinese Barbecue Sauce

Jerk Chicken • Grilled Turkey Burgers

Grilled Turkey Breast
with Tomato-Avocado Salsa

Grilled Burgers with Barbecued Red Onions

Greek-Style Lamb Burgers with Tzatziki

Skewered Beef Teriyaki

Herbed Garlic Shrimp

Don't let anyone put a glass of wine in your hands while you prepare the shrimp — they require your full attention because they cook very quickly. Brining shrimp guarantees they will remain moist when grilled.

Shrimp and Brine

- 6 cups water
- ½ cup salt
- ½ cup firmly packed light brown sugar
- 3 pounds jumbo shrimp (12 to 16 per pound)

Herb Sauce

- 1 cup coarsely chopped fresh parsley
- 1 cup fresh basil leaves
- 4 anchovy fillets, rinsed
- 4 garlic cloves

- 2 tablespoons drained capers
- 1 tablespoon grated lemon zest
- 2 tablespoons fresh lemon juice
- ⅔ cup extra-virgin olive oil
  Salt and freshly ground black pepper

Marinade

- ⅓ cup extra-virgin olive oil
- 3 tablespoons dry white wine
- 2 garlic cloves, minced
- 2 tablespoons chopped fresh parsley
- ¼ teaspoon crushed red pepper flakes

1. First, brine the shrimp. Stir together the water, salt, and brown sugar in a large bowl until the sugar dissolves. Add the shrimp. Refrigerate for at least 1 hour and up to 3 hours. Drain and rinse shrimp.

2. While the shrimp brines, prepare the sauce. Combine the parsley, basil, anchovy fillets, garlic, capers, lemon juice, and lemon zest in a food processor. With machine running, slowly blend in the oil. Season the sauce with salt and pepper. Set aside.

3. Next, butterfly the shrimp. Using a small, sharp knife, cut the shrimp in their shells along the full length of the back (do not cut all the way through). Remove the vein and pull off the legs. Open the shrimp and place in a large bowl.

4. Whisk the olive oil, white wine, garlic, parsley, and crushed red pepper in small bowl. Pour over the shrimp and stir gently to coat. Let stand for 30 minutes.

5. Prepare a medium-hot fire in a charcoal or gas grill.

6. When the coals are covered with white ash, place the shrimp, flesh side down, on the grill. Grill the shrimp until pink and cooked through, about 2 minutes per side.

7. Transfer the shrimp to a platter and serve, passing the sauce on the side.

SERVES 6

A VERSATILE HERB SAUCE   The dipping sauce is delicious but optional, because the shrimp are terrific on their own. If you do make the sauce, you might want to make a double batch. Not only is it great with the shrimp, it is also a delicious addition to any grilled fish or chicken.

Chicken Satay

Satays are made with meat, in this case chicken, threaded onto skewers, marinated, grilled, and served with a spicy peanut sauce. You can serve them as a main dish (in which case this recipe serves 6) or as an appetizer (which will serve as many as 24). As a main dish, satay is excellent served with rice and Thai Cabbage Salad (page 67).

Chicken and Marinade

- 3 pounds chicken tenders or boneless skinless chicken breasts
- ½ cup soy sauce
- ½ cup fresh lime juice
- 2 tablespoons crunchy peanut butter
- 1 tablespoon light brown sugar
- 1 tablespoon curry powder
- 2 garlic cloves, minced
- 1 teaspoon crushed red pepper flakes
- Chopped fresh peanuts

Peanut Sauce

- 1 (14-ounce) can unsweetened coconut milk
- ⅔ cups crunchy peanut butter
- ¼ cup fresh lime juice
- 2 tablespoons Asian fish sauce
- 2 tablespoons molasses
- 1 (1-inch piece) fresh ginger, peeled and minced
- 4 garlic cloves, minced
- Cayenne pepper
- ¼ cup finely chopped fresh cilantro

1. To prepare the chicken, arrange the chicken tenders on a large sheet of plastic wrap. Cover with a second sheet and pound with a meat mallet until about ¼ inch thick. Alternatively, slice the chicken breasts into strips about ½ inch wide and ¼ inch thick. Thread onto bamboo skewers and place in a large non-reactive baking pan.

2. To make the marinade, combine the soy sauce, lime juice, peanut butter, brown sugar, curry powder, garlic, and crushed red pepper in a blender and blend until smooth. Pour the marinade over the chicken skewers and refrigerate for at least 2 hours, or up to 8 hours, turning the skewers occasionally.

3. To make the peanut sauce, combine the coconut milk, peanut butter, lime juice, fish sauce, molasses, ginger, and garlic in a medium saucepan. Season to taste with cayenne pepper. Cook over medium heat, stirring constantly, until the sauce is smooth, about 5 minutes. Transfer to a blender and purée briefly. Add the cilantro and blend until smooth. (This mixture can be made several hours ahead and stored in the refrigerator. Bring to room temperature before serving.)

4. Prepare a medium-hot fire in a grill or preheat a broiler.

5. Grill or broil the skewered chicken, turning several times, until crispy on the outside but still moist on the inside, 4 to 6 minutes. Sprinkle the grilled chicken with the chopped peanuts. Serve hot, with the peanut sauce for dipping.

SERVES 6 TO 24

A Fresh Take on Leftovers

The flavorful leftover chicken is terrific in a wrap, especially when combined with the Thai Cabbage Salad (page 67).

Easy Side Dishes

Grilled Baked Potatoes

If you have the grill space, there is nothing simpler than wrapping Idaho or russet baking potatoes in foil, then baking over coals, and serving with butter and sour cream.

Be sure to scrub the potatoes and pierce each in several places with the tip of a sharp knife. Then wrap each potato in a double layer of aluminum foil. Mound all the coals on one side of the grill, or turn one burner off. Position the potatoes over the grill where there are no coals or over the burner that is off. Cover the grill and bake the potatoes until they are easily pierced with a knife, 45 to 60 minutes.

Grilled Garlic Bread

Grilled garlic bread is always a big hit, and goes well with just about every grilled meal, except burgers or hot dogs with buns. You can make a crowd-pleasing, garlicky bread a few different ways.

The conventional way to make a loaf of garlic bread is to slather sliced French or Italian bread with a mixture of melted butter and minced garlic, wrap the loaf in foil, and bake in a covered grill away from the hot coals or over a burner that is turned off, for about 10 minutes.

Alternatively, slice a loaf of bread in half horizontally. Brush the cut surface with a mixture of extra-virgin olive oil and minced garlic (about ¼ cup oil and 3 to 4 garlic cloves). Grill the bread over a medium-hot fire, cut sides up, until lightly toasted, about 4 minutes. Turn and grill the cut sides until lightly toasted, about 4 minutes more.

The fat-free method, which is surprisingly good, is to toast the bread over the coals and rub the cut surfaces with a garlic clove. This method only works with sturdy, artisanal bread that yields an uneven surface when sliced.

Grilled Corn

By grilling corn with their husks on, you provide enough steam to gently cook the corn and keep it moist. The charring of the husks adds even more flavor. Also, the husks will hold in the heat so you can hold the corn while you grill the meat portion of your meal. Buy the freshest corn you can, preferably picked on the day you will serve it.

To prepare the corn, pull off the dry outer husks until you get to the tender light green inner ones; leave these on. Save a few husks and tear into ¼-inch strips and set aside. Pull the inner husks back gently and remove the silk. Baste the ears with butter or oil, then close and tie with the reserved strips. Place the corn on the grill and cover. Grill, turning occasionally, for 15 to 20 minutes, until the husks are streaked with brown. Just before serving, remove the husks, a messy job that is best done outdoors.

Simple Grilled Chicken

The secret to great grilled chicken is to bank all the coals on one side of the grill, place a drip pan on the other side, and arrange the chicken on the grill above the drip pan. The chicken will grill to perfection, without the dreaded flare-ups that can leave grilled chicken charred on the outside and raw inside.

Juice of 1 lemon
2 tablespoons extra-virgin olive oil
2 large garlic cloves, minced
1 teaspoon minced fresh rosemary or thyme
2 teaspoons salt
¼ teaspoon freshly ground black pepper
3- to 4-pound chicken, cut up, or 3 to 4 pounds chicken parts

1. Whisk together the lemon juice, oil, garlic, rosemary, salt, and pepper in a small bowl. Rub the mixture all over the chicken pieces, tucking some of it under the skin. Allow to marinate in the refrigerator, covered, for 1 to 4 hours.

2. Prepare a hot fire in a gas or charcoal grill.

3. When the coals in the charcoal grill are covered with gray ash, push all the coals to one side of the grill and place a drip pan on the other side. Or turn off one side of the gas grill and place the drip pan over the off burner. If desired, add wood chips according to the manufacturer's directions.

4. Lightly oil the grill. Place the chicken skin side up on the grate over the drip pan. Cover the grill and grill for 45 to 60 minutes, until the juices run clear and the chicken shows no pink against the bone.

5. Remove from grill and serve hot or cold.

SERVES 4 TO 6

GRILLING TIP   If you are making chicken for a big crowd, you will need to run two grills simultaneously or grill serially. A standard 22-inch Webber kettle grill will hold the parts of two small chickens, so multiply the recipe as needed. Use a charcoal chimney to light the coals for a second batch of chicken once the first batch is about half done.

Food is our common ground, a universal experience.

—JAMES BEARD

Grilled Chicken Wings with Chinese Barbecue Sauce

The odd thing is that 5-pound bags of chicken wings can contain as many as sixty pieces and as few as thirty. Look for bags filled with bigger pieces; big pieces cook better, are easier to handle on the grill, and most people prefer their meatiness. The chicken wings are often labeled "second section," meaning the wing-tips are removed and the drumettes are separated from the wing sections.

1   (5-pound) bag chicken wings, defrosted and patted dry
3   tablespoons Asian sesame oil
1   tablespoon soy sauce
2   garlic cloves, minced
1   (1-inch piece) fresh ginger, peeled and minced
½   cup hoisin sauce

1. Prepare a medium-hot fire in a charcoal grill with the coals under half the grill only and a drip pan placed next to the coals. In a gas grill, preheat the grill on high, then reduce one side of the gas grill to medium and turn the other side off.

2. Combine the chicken pieces, sesame oil, soy sauce, garlic, and ginger in a large bowl and toss to coat.

3. Place the chicken over the hot coals and grill for 4 to 5 minutes on both sides, until the chicken is browned.

4. Brush the wings with the hoisin sauce and move to the side of the grill over the drip pan. Continue to grill, basting and turning a few times, until the chicken is well browned and cooked through, 12 to 15 minutes more.

5. Serve hot or at room temperature.

MAKES 30 TO 60 PIECES

Potluck Pick

Chicken wings disappear quickly from a potluck spread, picnic table, or appetizer tray. The recipe is easily doubled, but it will require careful grilling to avoid flare-ups. Hoisin sauce is readily found in the Asian ingredients aisle of most supermarkets.

Jerk Chicken

Someone once described jerk as a festival of flavors in the mouth, and that's about as good a description of this chicken as any. The chicken is sweet, spicy, and hot all at the same time; it is a riot of flavors that everyone will enjoy. Don't be put off by the long list of ingredients; this is very easy to make.

6 garlic cloves

4 fresh Scotch bonnet or habanero chiles, seeded

4 scallions

1 small onion

1 tablespoon fresh thyme leaves

¼ cup fresh lime juice

3 tablespoons extra-virgin olive oil

3 tablespoons soy sauce

1 tablespoon salt

1 tablespoon packed light or dark brown sugar

2 teaspoons ground allspice

2 teaspoons freshly ground black pepper

1½ teaspoons ground cinnamon

½ teaspoon freshly grated nutmeg

3 chicken breast halves (with skin and bones), halved crosswise

3 to 4 pounds bone-in chicken thighs

1. To make the marinade, combine the garlic, chiles, scallions, onion, and thyme in a food processor and process until finely chopped. Add the lime juice, oil, soy sauce, salt, brown sugar, allspice, black pepper, cinnamon, and nutmeg, and process until well blended.

2. Arrange the chicken pieces in a large roasting pan. Add the marinade, turning to coat the chicken. Cover and marinate in the refrigerator for at least 2 and up to 8 hours, turning once or twice.

3. Prepare a hot fire in a gas or charcoal grill.

4. When the coals in the charcoal grill are covered with gray ash, push all the coals to one side of the grill and place a drip pan on the other side. Or turn off one side of the gas grill and place the drip pan over the off burner. If desired, add wood chips according to the manufacturer's directions.

5. Lightly oil the grill. Place the chicken skin side up on the grate over the drip pan. Cover the grill and grill for 45 to 60 minutes, until the juices run clear and the chicken shows no pink against the bone.

6. Remove from grill and serve hot or cold.

SERVES 6 TO 8

He who receives his friends and gives no personal attention to the meal which is being prepared for them, is not worthy of having friends.

—JEAN-ANTHELME BRILLAT-SAVARIN
WRITING IN *THE PHYSIOLOGY OF TASTE*

The Sandwich Solution

Sandwiches are always crowd-pleasers at casual parties — from picnics to Super Bowl parties to graduation teas.

The best thing about sandwiches is that they are easy to prepare for, easy to eat, and involve relatively little in the way of cleanup. Preparation can be done one day in advance if you have the space for trays in your refrigerator.

In addition to platters of deli meats and sliced cheese, offer a full array of condiments and relishes. Besides the obvious mustard, mayonnaise, and butter, include an Italian olive salad or artichoke relish to add to the sandwiches. Offer a platter of sliced tomatoes, shredded lettuce, sliced red onions, and pickles. A varied selection of bread and sandwich rolls rounds out the presentation.

When calculating amounts to buy, figure that each sandwich maker will probably take 4 ounces of meats and cheese and 1½ tablespoons of dressing (mayo or mustard).

Grilled Turkey Burgers

Tired of the same old burgers every time you organize a cookout? These turkey burgers are guaranteed crowd-pleasers, and a more healthful alternative to ground beef. Pass ketchup and mustard at the table, as well as lettuce and sliced tomatoes, but don't be surprised that some will prefer these burgers plain.

2¼ **pounds ground turkey**	2 **teaspoons Worcestershire sauce**
½ **cup chopped scallions**	1 **teaspoon salt**
¼ **cup chopped fresh parsley**	½ **teaspoon freshly ground black pepper**
1 **tablespoon chopped fresh oregano, or 1 teaspoon dried**	8 **onion rolls or hamburger buns**
2 **garlic cloves, minced**	

1. Combine the turkey with the scallions, parsley, oregano, garlic, Worcestershire sauce, salt, and pepper in a large bowl. Mix well. Form into eight 1-inch-thick patties.

2. Prepare a medium-hot fire in a charcoal or gas grill.

3. Grill the patties until cooked through, about 6 minutes per side, turning once. While the patties grill, grill the buns, cut side down, until lightly toasted, about 2 minutes.

4. To serve, place the patties on the bottom halves of the buns. Cover each with a bun top. Serve at once.

SERVES 8

Grilled Turkey Breast with Tomato-Avocado Salsa

The great thing about cooking a turkey breast is that you can avoid overcooking, which frequently happens when you cook the whole bird. Grilling the breasts with a spicy rub seals in the flavor and the moisture. A bright salsa of tomatoes and avocado finishes the dish and makes it a real crowd-pleaser. This recipe requires presoaked wood chips to add a smoky flavor to the turkey, so be sure to set wood chips in water about 30 minutes before you plan to cook.

Turkey

- 2 tablespoons chili powder
- 2 tablespoons sugar
- 1 teaspoon ground cumin
- 1 teaspoon coarse sea salt
- 1 teaspoon garlic powder
- ½ teaspoon ground allspice
- 2 (3-pound) split turkey breasts

Salsa

- 3 cups ripe tomatoes, seeded and diced
- 2 ripe avocados, peeled, pitted, and diced
- 1 jalapeño, seeded and diced
- ¼ cup finely chopped red onion or sweet onion, such as Vidalia
- 2 tablespoons chopped fresh cilantro
- Juice of 1 large lime
- Salt and freshly ground black pepper

1. Combine the chili powder, sugar, cumin, salt, garlic powder, and allspice in a small bowl; mix well. Rub the mixture into the two turkey breast halves. Set aside.

2. Prepare a hot fire in a gas or charcoal grill.

3. When the coals in the charcoal grill are covered with gray ash, push all the coals to one side of the grill and place a drip pan on the other side. Or turn off one side of the gas grill and place the drip pan over the off burner. Add presoaked wood chips.

4. When the grill is ready, place the turkey skin side up over the drip pan, on the side away from the direct heat. Add the soaked wood chips directly to a charcoal fire or according to the manufacturer's direction in a gas grill. Cover the grill and grill the turkey for 1 to 1½ hours, until the temperature in an instant-read thermometer inserted into the thickest part of the breast registers 160°F.

5. While the turkey grills, make the salsa. Combine the tomatoes, avocados, jalapeño, onion, cilantro, and lime juice in a medium bowl. Season to taste with salt and pepper. Toss gently.

6. When the turkey is done, remove from the heat and let rest under an aluminum foil tent for 10 minutes.

7. Carve the turkey and serve with the salsa on the side.

SERVES 8

The only real stumbling block is fear of failure. In cooking you've got to have a what-the-hell attitude.

—JULIA CHILD

Grilled Burgers with Barbecued Red Onions

Can an all-beef grilled hamburger be improved upon? When you're in the mood for a hamburger, nothing else can compare. But adding caramelized, grilled onions is a lovely touch, as is substituting buffalo meat or turkey for a lower fat profile. A combination of ground buffalo and ground turkey is particularly pleasing.

3   pounds ground beef or buffalo meat, or 1½ pounds ground buffalo meat and 1½ pounds ground turkey

2   tablespoons ketchup

2   teaspoons salt

1   teaspoon freshly ground black pepper

8   (½-inch-thick) slices red onions

½   cup bottled barbecue sauce

8   hamburger buns, split

1. Prepare a medium-hot fire in a charcoal or gas grill.

2. Combine the ground meat, ketchup, salt, and pepper in a large bowl and mix well. Form the burgers into eight 4- to 5-inch diameter patties.

3. Brush the onions generously with the barbecue sauce. Place on the grill and grill until the onions are tender, brown, and glazed, basting with barbecue sauce and turning occasionally, about 15 minutes. Remove to a plate and keep warm.

4. Grill the patties until cooked through, 3 to 5 minutes per side, turning once. While the patties grill, grill hamburger buns, cut side down, until lightly toasted, about 2 minutes.

5. To serve, place the patties on the bottom halves of the buns. Top each with an onion slice, then with the bun tops. Serve at once.

SERVES 8

Better Burgers

- Never press burgers with the spatula as they grill. Pressing squeezes out the juices and results in dry meat.

- When making beef burgers, buy 85 percent lean ground round. Ground chuck is too fatty, and ground sirloin too lean.

- Every crowd is sure to include a vegetarian these days. Have some soy or garden burgers in the freezer if you aren't positive all your guests eat meat.

- Consider offering ground buffalo meat for a low-fat alternative to beef. The flavor is excellent, and your healthy-living friends will be touched by your thoughtfulness.

- Add extra flavor to your burgers by serving them on good-quality sourdough or hard rolls.

Wine Choices for Grilled Foods

Beer is the obvious choice when serving burgers and other casual fare off the grill. But if you prefer wine, there are many good options.

Steaks and beef burgers pair well with medium-bodied red wines, such as Bordeaux, Cabernet Franc, Côtes-du-Rhône reds, Merlot, Grenache, and Pinot Noir. Grilled steaks also go well with rich, dense tannic reds, such as Barbaresco, Barolo, California Cabernet, or Australian Shiraz.

Grilled chicken pairs nicely with most whites. Grilled tofu and grilled vegetables pair well with most whites or a light, fruity red, such as Beaujolais, Nebbiola, Sangiovese, and most rosés.

Greek-Style Lamb Burgers with Tzatziki

These lamb burgers are designed to have the flavor of those delicious gyros one finds at Greek diners, in the convenient form of lamb patties. The garlicky cucumber relish, tzatziki, that accompanies the lamb is the quintessential condiment. A Greek salad or tomato salad makes a fine accompaniment, as do oven-roasted potatoes.

Tzatziki

- 6 cups quartered very thinly sliced cucumbers (peeled and seeded if necessary)
- 1 teaspoon salt, or more as needed
- 4 cups full-fat Greek yogurt, or 2 cups sour cream and 2 cups plain yogurt
- 2 garlic cloves, minced
  Freshly ground black pepper

Burgers

- 2 garlic cloves, peeled
- 3 tablespoons mint leaves, or 1 tablespoon dried
- 2 tablespoons fresh oregano leaves, or 1 tablespoon dried
- 2 teaspoons salt
- 1 teaspoon freshly ground black pepper
- 2 pounds ground lamb
- 6 pita pockets, cut in halves

1. To make the tzatziki, combine the cucumbers and 1 teaspoon of the salt in a colander and toss to mix. Let drain for 30 to 60 minutes. Transfer the cucumbers to a clean kitchen towel and pat dry.

2. Combine the cucumbers, yogurt, and garlic. Season generously with the pepper and more salt, if desired. Set aside at room temperature to allow the flavors to develop.

3. Prepare a medium-hot fire in the barbecue.

4. To make the burgers, combine the garlic, mint, oregano, salt, and pepper in a food processor. Process until finely chopped. Add the lamb and pulse until well mixed; do not overprocess. Form the meat mixture into twelve small patties.

5. Wrap the pita pockets in aluminum foil.

6. When the coals are covered with white ash, place the pita pockets on the grill away from the coals. Grill the lamb patties over the hot coals, until cooked through, about 4 minutes per side for medium, turning once.

8. Serve the patties hot, passing the pita pockets and tzatziki on the side, letting your guests make their own sandwiches.

SERVES 6

Advance Preparations

The tzatziki can be made up to 8 hours in advance, and the lamb mixture can be mixed and made into patties up to 8 hours in advance and refrigerated. Grill the burgers just before serving.

Traditional Clambake

If you have an outdoor fire pit and summer weather, consider a clambake for your next gathering. If you can throw in a beach, even better.

The early American settlers found an abundance of seafood all along the Atlantic coast. In New England, settlers learned from the Native Americans how to bake shellfish in fire pits packed with seaweed. Often lobster is baked along with the clams, although gone are the days when the going price for lobster was twenty-five cents for a dozen (in the eighteenth century). Today, the fire pits may contain clams, lobsters, mussels, corn, potatoes, and sausages. There are really no rules.

Allow about 1 quart of clams in the shell per person, 1 lobster per person, 1 to 2 ears of corn per person.

To make the fire pit, dig a large pit in the sand (or in the ground) at least 1 foot deep. Line the pit with stones and build a wood fire on the stones. Allow the fire to burn down. After 1 hour, when the stones are white hot, you are ready to cook.

Scrub the clams in seawater or under cold running water. Kill the lobsters by inserting a sharp, heavy knife into the lobster where the head meets the body, so they don't walk off the fire. Dip the corn in seawater or salted tap water.

Sweep the ashes off the rocks and cover the rocks with a thin layer of seaweed. Place a piece of chicken wire or a grill rack over the seaweed. Pile the clams, lobsters, and corn on top. Cover with more seaweed, then a piece of canvas to hold in the steam. Steam for 1 hour.

Serve with plenty of melted butter and paper napkins. No eating utensils required.

Skewered Beef Teriyaki

The tasty beef strips will disappear quickly, especially when served as appetizers, coming hot off the grill before the main course. As a main dish, they will serve six, with rice and an assortment of vegetable sides.

2 pounds boneless steak, cut into ¼-inch thick strips across the grain

¼ cup soy sauce

¼ cup dry sherry or rice wine

2 tablespoons orange juice

1 tablespoon sugar

1 tablespoon peeled and minced fresh ginger

2 scallions, white and tender green parts, minced

2 garlic cloves, minced

1. Put the meat in a large heavy-duty resealable plastic bag or shallow baking dish.

2. Whisk together the soy sauce, sherry, orange juice, sugar, ginger, scallions, and garlic in a small bowl. Pour the marinade over meat. Cover and refrigerate for at least 4 and up to 8 hours.

3. Prepare a hot fire in a gas or charcoal grill.

4. Thread the meat onto the skewers.

5. Grill briefly over the hot coals, 1 to 2 minutes per side, turning once.

6. Serve hot.

MAKES ABOUT 30 SKEWERS

SIMPLE SLICING You might consider buying more steak than you need and trimming the beef to make an even rectangle shape. All the slices will be more or less the same size, and the trimmings can be used in a stir-fry. Also keep in mind that steak is easier to slice when it is partially frozen.

7 • Desserts & Bake Sales

Cookie Pops • Snowballs

Triple Chocolate Chip Cookies

Peanut Butter–Chocolate Kiss Cookies

Brownie Pizza

Chocolate-Raspberry Brownies

One-Bowl Chocolate Cupcakes

Golden Sheet Cake with Chocolate Frosting

One-Pot Chocolate Cake

Pound Cake • Strawberry Cheesecake

Apple-Raspberry Crisp

Fresh Fruit Tart

Praline Ice-Cream Pie

Chocolate Mint Ice-Cream Pie

Cookie Pops

These cookies fly off the bake sale table when there are small children around. But they are fragile, so take care when handling and transporting them. You will need three dozen wooden Popsicle sticks, also called craft sticks, for turning the cookies into lollipops.

3¾	cups sifted unbleached all-purpose flour	1	cup (2 sticks) lightly salted butter, at room temperature
4½	teaspoons baking powder	2	large eggs
¼	teaspoon salt	2½	teaspoons vanilla extract
2	cups granulated sugar		Confectioners' sugar, for dusting
			Decorating icing

1. Stir together the flour, baking powder, and salt in a medium bowl.

2. Cream together the sugar, butter, eggs, and vanilla in a large mixing bowl with an electric mixer on medium-high speed until light and fluffy. Scrape down the sides of the bowl. Add the flour, in three batches, beating on low speed after each addition. Form the dough into two balls, flatten the balls, wrap in plastic wrap, and refrigerate for 20 minutes.

3. Preheat the oven to 350°F. Line two large baking sheets with parchment paper.

4. On a surface lightly dusted with confectioners' sugar, roll out the dough to a thickness of slightly more than ⅛ inch. Cut out the cookies with 3½-inch round or animal-shaped cutters. Place the cookies ½ inch apart on the prepared cookie sheets. Insert a craft stick ¾ inch deep into the bottom of each cookie.

5. Bake, one sheet at a time, for 7 to 9 minutes, or until lightly browned. Very carefully transfer the cookies to a rack and let cool.

6. Using decorating icing, draw faces or other designs on the cooled cookies.

MAKES ABOUT 36

Snowballs

If it's December, call these Christmas snowdrops or snowballs; other times of the year, you may know these sugar-coated buttery balls of nuts as Russian tea cakes, Mexican wedding cakes, Italian butter nuts, Southern pecan butterballs, or Viennese sugar balls.

1 cup pecans, walnuts, or hazelnuts	½ teaspoon vanilla extract
2 cups confectioners' sugar	2 cups unbleached all-purpose flour
1 cup (2 sticks) butter, at room temperature	½ teaspoon salt

1. Combine the nuts and 1 cup of the confectioners' sugar in a food processor. Process until the nuts are finely ground. Add the butter and vanilla, and beat until light and fluffy. Beat in the flour and salt until combined. Cover and refrigerate the dough for about 1 hour, or until firm.

2. Preheat the oven to 350°F. Line two cookie sheets with parchment paper.

3. Form the dough into 1-inch balls and place 2 inches apart on the prepared cookie sheets.

4. Bake for 15 to 20 minutes, until lightly browned.

5. While the cookies are baking, place the remaining 1 cup confectioners' sugar in a shallow bowl.

6. Cool the cookies on the parchment sheets for a few minutes. While still warm, roll the cookies in the confectioners' sugar. Place on a wire rack to cool.

7. When the cookies have cooled, roll them again in the confectioners' sugar to give them an even coating of sugar. Store in an airtight container between sheets of parchment or waxed paper. They will keep well for at least 1 week.

MAKES ABOUT 36

Triple Chocolate Chip Cookies

Chocolate chip cookies are very popular, and you can be sure someone will be bringing some to your next bake sale. Make your cookies special by intensifying the chocolate experience.

4 ounces unsweetened chocolate, coarsely chopped

4 ounces bittersweet chocolate, coarsely chopped

½ cup (1 stick) butter, cut into pieces

1 cup unbleached all-purpose flour

½ teaspoon baking powder

½ teaspoon salt

3 large eggs

1¼ cups firmly packed light or dark brown sugar

2 teaspoons vanilla extract

1 cup white chocolate chips

1 cup pecan pieces, chopped

½ cup granulated sugar

1. Melt the unsweetened chocolate, bittersweet chocolate, and butter in the top of a double boiler set over simmering water. Stir until completely smooth and glossy. Remove the top of the double boiler from the heat and let cool slightly.

2. Whisk together the flour, baking powder, and salt in a medium bowl.

3. Beat the eggs and brown sugar in a large bowl with an electric mixer set at medium-high speed until very thick, about 4 minutes. Beat in the vanilla until well mixed. Reduce the speed to low and add the chocolate mixture. Beat until well mixed.

4. Fold in the flour with a large rubber spatula. Fold in the white chocolate chips and nuts. Cover the bowl and let stand at room temperature for 30 minutes to stiffen the batter.

5. Preheat the oven to 350°F. Line three baking sheets with parchment paper. Place the granulated sugar in a shallow bowl.

6. Using a 1½-ounce ice-cream scoop or a tablespoon, form the cookie dough into walnut-size balls and roll in the granulated sugar. Place about 2 inches apart on the cookie sheets.

7. Bake the cookies, one sheet at a time, on the middle rack of the oven for 12 to 14 minutes. Transfer the sheets to racks and cool the cookies before removing them.

MAKES ABOUT 36

Advance Preparations

These cookies age well in an airtight container. Feel free to make them several days in advance. They will keep for up to a week.

TIP

Bake Sale Success

- Tailor your offerings to the event. Cupcakes and cookies sell well at schools, but for an adult clientele, think pies, cakes, pastries, loaves of bread, even jars of jam.

- Presentation is everything. A pretty box, a paper doily under a plate of cookies, a cake encircled by edible flowers — small touches announce that the baker took pride in her offering.

- Never take foods to a bake sale in containers you want back.

- Cover everything with clear plastic wrap and provide labels.

Peanut Butter–Chocolate Kiss Cookies

With the purchase of a bag of Kiss candies, you convert a simple peanut butter cookie into an irresistible treat. Watch these disappear.

¾ cup smooth peanut butter

½ cup (1 stick) butter, softened

½ cup firmly packed dark or light brown sugar

½ cup granulated sugar

1 large egg

1 teaspoon vanilla extract

1½ cups unbleached all-purpose flour

1 teaspoon baking powder

½ teaspoon baking soda

½ teaspoon ground cinnamon

Approximately 36 chocolate kisses, unwrapped

1. Preheat the oven to 350°F.

2. Combine the peanut butter, butter, brown sugar, and granulated sugar in a food processor and process until well blended. Add egg and vanilla and process until well blended. Add the flour, baking powder, baking soda, and cinnamon and process until the dough comes together. The dough should be soft enough to hold together in a ball.

3. Pinch off walnut-size chunks of dough and roll in your hands to form smooth balls. Place about 2 inches apart on ungreased baking sheets.

4. Bake one sheet at a time for 8 to 9 minutes, until the cookies are just barely done. Remove from the oven and immediately press a chocolate kiss in the center of each cookie, pressing gently. The cookies will crack but not break. Return to the oven to bake for 1 minute more. Let the cookies cool on the baking sheet for at least 5 minutes before removing them to finish cooling on racks. Repeat with the remaining cookies.

MAKES ABOUT 36

Brownie Pizza

The most successful brownie pizzas are the ones that try to mimic real pizza, with grated white chocolate standing in for the mozzarella. Thin rounds of red licorice can simulate pepperoni and thin strips of leaf-shaped green jelly candies can stand in for strips of green peppers. An aluminum foil pizza pan is convenient for baking and packaging the pizza.

¾ cup (1½ sticks) butter, cut up

4½ ounces unsweetened chocolate

2 cups sugar

3 large eggs, lightly beaten

1 tablespoon vanilla extract

1½ cups unbleached all-purpose flour

2 ounces white chocolate

½ cup assorted candies (jelly beans, sliced gumdrops, sliced licorice, etc.)

1. Preheat the oven to 350°F. Butter a 12-inch aluminum pizza pan. If you are using a regular pizza pan, line with parchment paper cut 4 inches larger than the pan, for ease of moving the pizza.

2. Combine the butter and chocolate in the top of a double boiler over simmering water and melt, stirring frequently. Let cool for 1 minute.

3. Stir the sugar, eggs, and vanilla into the melted butter mixture. Stir in the flour until smooth. Pour into the prepared pan and spread evenly with a spatula.

4. Bake for about 18 minutes, until the top springs back when touched lightly.

5. While the brownie bakes, grate the white chocolate on the largest side of a grater. Sprinkle the grated chocolate over the hot brownie and top with the candies. Let cool in the pan. To serve, cut into 12 wedges using a large knife or pizza wheel.

MAKES 12 SLICES

Chocolate-Raspberry Brownies

Although nothing tastes better than a gooey, still-warm brownie, when you are baking for a bake sale the secret is to make the brownies one day ahead. Brownies that have sat in the pan overnight will cut cleanly and neatly; brownies made a few hours earlier will not. Raspberry jam perfumes these rich chocolatey brownies with a hint of raspberry.

1 cup (2 sticks) butter, cut up	½ cup raspberry jam
4 ounces unsweetened chocolate	1 teaspoon vanilla extract
4 large eggs	¼ teaspoon salt
1 cup sugar	1 cup unbleached all-purpose flour

1. Preheat the oven to 350°F. Butter a 9- by 13-inch baking pan. Line the pan with aluminum foil, allowing the ends to overlap the ends of the pan by several inches. Butter the aluminum foil.

2. Melt the chocolate and butter in a heavy-bottomed saucepan, over low heat, stirring until smooth. Let cool to room temperature.

3. Beat the eggs in a large bowl until light and fluffy. Slowly beat in the sugar until the mixture is light and fluffy. Beat in the jam, vanilla, and salt. Add the chocolate mixture and beat until smooth. Fold in the flour. Spoon the batter into the prepared pan.

4. Bake for about 25 minutes, or until the top feels dry and looks shiny. The inside will be soft, but will firm up when cooled.

5. Cool the brownies completely in the pan on a rack.

6. Lift the brownies out of the pan by holding onto the ends of the aluminum foil. Peel off the aluminum foil. Cut the brownies into squares.

MAKES 12 TO 16 BROWNIES

One-Bowl Chocolate Cupcakes

Here's a recipe so easy, so foolproof, so quick to make that it is perfect for those times when your child lets you know at bedtime that you have been volunteered for the next day's bake sale.

Cupcakes

- 1¼ cups unbleached all-purpose flour
- ¾ cup granulated sugar
- 3 tablespoons unsweetened cocoa powder
- 1½ teaspoons baking powder
- ½ teaspoon salt
- ¾ cup water
- ¼ cup vegetable oil
- 1 teaspoon vanilla extract
- ¼ cup white chocolate or semisweet chips

Fudge Frosting

- ¼ cup (½ stick) butter, at room temperature
- 1½ ounces cream cheese, at room temperature
- ¾ cup confectioners' sugar
- 2 tablespoons unsweetened cocoa powder
- 1 teaspoon vanilla extract
- Sprinkles, colored sugar crystals, miniature candies, etc., for garnish

1. Preheat the oven to 350°F. Line a 12-cup muffin tin with twelve paper liners.

2. To make the cupcakes, sift together the flour, granulated sugar, cocoa, baking powder, and salt into a medium mixing bowl. In a glass measuring cup, combine the water, oil, and vanilla. Make a well in the dry ingredients and pour in the liquids. Mix well. Stir in the chocolate chips. Spoon the batter into the muffin cups, filling them halfway.

3. Bake for 18 to 20 minutes, until a cake tester inserted in the center of one of the cupcakes comes out clean.

4. Cool on a rack in the pan for about 10 minutes. Remove the cupcakes from the tin and finish cooling on the rack.

5. To make the frosting, combine the butter and cream cheese in a food processor and process until smooth. Add the confectioners' sugar, cocoa, and vanilla, and continue to process until smooth.

6. Frost the cupcakes and decorate with a garnish.

MAKES 12

THE PERFECT FINISH   When decorating cupcakes for kids, nothing pleases more than candy. To decorate for grown-ups, melt ½ cup of white chocolate chips in a microwave and drizzle over the cakes with the tines of a fork.

The true essentials of a feast are only fun and feed.

OLIVER WENDELL HOLMES, SR.

Golden Sheet Cake with Chocolate Frosting

A gold cake with dark chocolate frosting makes a classic birthday cake — big enough to serve to a whole class, the whole office, or any large gathering.

Cake

- 4½ cups sifted unbleached all-purpose flour
- 1½ tablespoons baking powder
- 1½ teaspoons salt
- 1½ cups (3 sticks) butter, at room temperature
- 2¼ cups sugar
- 1 tablespoon vanilla extract
- 8 whole eggs, plus 8 egg yolks
- 1¼ cups milk

Chocolate Frosting

- ½ cup (1 stick) butter, cut up
- 4 ounces unsweetened chocolate
- 2 ounces semisweet or dark chocolate
- 2 teaspoons vanilla extract
- 4 cups sifted confectioners' sugar
- 4–6 tablespoons milk or cream

1. Preheat the oven to 350°F. Butter and flour an 11- by 15-inch sheet pan.

2. Sift together the flour, baking powder, and salt. Set aside.

3. In a large mixing bowl, beat the butter until creamy. Gradually add the sugar and vanilla, beating until fluffy.

4. Beat the eggs and egg yolks in a medium bowl until thick and lemon colored. Add to the butter mixture. (If you are using an electric mixer, add the eggs and egg yolks to the butter mixture one at a time, beating thoroughly after each addition.)

5. Add about one-quarter of the dry ingredients to the creamed mixture, beating until blended, then add a third of the milk. Repeat the procedure, alternating the flour and milk, ending with the flour. Mix just until batter is smooth and blended. Scrape the batter into the prepared pan.

6. Bake for 35 to 45 minutes, until a cake tester inserted in center of cake comes out clean.

7. Cool on a wire rack.

8. To make the frosting, melt the butter and chocolates in a heavy saucepan over low heat. Remove from the heat, add the vanilla, and stir until smooth. Transfer to a mixing bowl and let cool slightly. Gradually add half of the confectioners' sugar, beating thoroughly. Beat in 2 tablespoons of the cream, then the remaining confectioners' sugar. Add enough cream to make a smooth frosting of spreading consistency. Spread the frosting on the cooled cake.

SERVES 32

One-Pot Chocolate Cake

A cake you can put together in 10 minutes is a worthy addition to your repertoire. The chocolate cake looks lovely with the white glaze.

Cake

- 1 cup (2 sticks) butter, cut up
- 4 ounces semisweet or bittersweet chocolate
- 3 large eggs
- 2 cups sugar
- 1 teaspoon vanilla extract
- 2½ cups unbleached all-purpose flour
- 1 tablespoon baking powder
- 1 teaspoon baking soda
- 1 teaspoon salt
- 1 cup cold coffee

Glaze

- 2 ounces white chocolate
- 1 tablespoon butter

1. Preheat the oven to 350°F. Butter and flour a 10-inch tube or Bundt pan.

2. To make the cake, melt the butter with the chocolate in a heavy-bottomed saucepan. Remove from the heat and beat in the eggs, sugar, and vanilla. Sift together the flour, baking powder, baking soda, and salt. Mix together lightly, then mix into the batter. Stir in the coffee. Scrape the batter into the prepared pan.

3. Bake for about 50 minutes, until a cake tester inserted near the center comes out clean.

4. Cool the cake in the pan on a wire rack for about 15 minutes. Loosen the edges; invert onto a rack to cool completely.

5. To make the glaze, melt the white chocolate with the butter in the top of a double boiler set over simmering water or in a microwave. Whisk until the chocolate is smooth. Drizzle over the cake in a decorative pattern, letting the chocolate drip off the tines of a fork. Let the icing set at room temperature for at least 15 minutes before serving.

SERVES 16

Pound Cake

Pound cakes are ideal for entertaining because they can be made ahead, cooled, and wrapped in plastic wrap, then foil. Wrapped cakes will keep for about 3 days at room temperature, for 1 week in the refrigerator, or up to 2 months in the freezer. They can be served plain, dusted with confectioners' sugar, glazed with melted chocolate, or served with a fruit compote, sliced peaches, or ice cream.

4 cups sifted cake flour	1½ cups sugar
½ teaspoon salt	10 large eggs, at room temperature
2 cups (4 sticks) butter, at room temperature	4 teaspoons vanilla extract

1. Preheat the oven to 325°F. Grease and flour two 9- by 5-inch loaf pans.

2. Sift the flour and salt into a medium bowl.

3. Cream the butter until light and fluffy in a large mixing bowl with an electric mixer. Add the sugar gradually, beating continuously for 5 minutes, until the mixture is fluffy. Beat in the eggs one at a time, beating well after each addition. Add the vanilla. Fold in the dry ingredients, mixing until the batter is smooth and blended. Pour into the prepared pans. Shake the pans to level the batter.

4. Bake for 55 to 65 minutes, until a cake tester inserted in the center of each cake comes out clean.

5. Let the cakes cool on a rack for 10 minutes. Remove the cakes from the pans and let cool completely.

SERVES 24

Strawberry Cheesecake

Cheesecakes are special-occasion cakes; they are simply too rich to offer as an everyday dessert, but everyone loves them. With a topping of glossy strawberries, this cheesecake is an impressive beauty that requires no special skills on the part of the baker.

Crust

- 1½ cups finely ground graham cracker crumbs (from 1 packet graham crackers)
- 3 tablespoons sugar
- 6 tablespoons butter, melted
- ¼ teaspoon ground cinnamon

Cheese Filling

- 2½ pounds cream cheese (five 8-ounce packages), at room temperature
- 1¾ cups sugar
- 3 tablespoons unbleached all-purpose flour
- 2 teaspoons finely grated lemon zest
- 2 teaspoons freshly squeezed lemon juice
- 1 teaspoon vanilla extract
- ¼ cup milk
- 5 large eggs plus 2 large egg yolks

Topping

- ¼ cup strawberry jelly
- 1 pound fresh strawberries, hulled and halved lengthwise

1. Preheat the oven to 350°F. Lightly grease a 9-inch springform pan.

2. To make the crust, combine the graham cracker crumbs, sugar, butter, and cinnamon in a medium bowl and mix until well combined. Press firmly into the bottom and up the sides of the pan.

3. Bake for 8 minutes. Reduce the oven to 325°F. Set aside on a rack to cool before filling.

4. To make the cheese filling, combine the cream cheese, sugar, flour, lemon zest, lemon juice, and vanilla in a large mixing bowl by hand or on the lowest speed, if using an electric mixer, until it is creamy and smooth. Beat together the milk, eggs, and egg yolks in a small bowl. Beat into the cream cheese mixture just until smooth. Pour the cheese mixture into the crust-lined pan.

5. Bake the cake for 1 to 1¼ hours, until the center appears set. The cake will become firm as it chills. Turn off the oven and let the cake cool in the oven.

6. Gently run a sharp knife around the edge of pan. Refrigerate until thoroughly chilled.

7. To make the topping, stir the jelly in heavy saucepan over low heat until melted. Arrange the berry halves atop cheesecake in concentric circles; brush with warm jelly to glaze. Chill for at least 1 hour and up to 8 hours.

SERVES 16

Without the assistance of eating and drinking, the most sparkling wit would be as heavy as a bad soufflé, and the brightest talent as dull as a looking-glass on a foggy day.

ALEXIS SOYER, 19TH-CENTURY FRENCH CHEF, WRITING IN *THE MODERN HOUSEWIFE* (1851)

Apple-Raspberry Crisp

Raspberry jam infuses the apples with delicate flavor and a beautiful rosy color. This is a quick dessert to throw together for a casual gathering.

Filling

- 12 cups peeled and sliced apples (10 to 12 apples)
- ¾ cup raspberry jam
- 2 tablespoons fresh lemon juice
- ½ teaspoon ground cinnamon

Topping

- 1¼ cups granola (preferably without raisins)
- 1 cup old-fashioned rolled oats

- ½ cup unbleached all-purpose flour
- ½ cup packed light or dark brown sugar
- 2 teaspoons ground cinnnamon
- ½ cup (1 stick) butter, at room temperature
- ¾ cup chopped nuts (almonds, pecans, or walnuts)

Cream, whipped cream, or ice cream, to serve

1. Preheat the oven to 350°F. Butter a 9- by 13-inch baking dish.

2. To make the filling, combine the apples in a large bowl with the jam, lemon juice, and cinnamon. Toss gently to mix. Transfer the apples to the prepared baking dish.

3. To make the topping, combine the granola, oats, flour, brown sugar, and cinnamon. With your fingers or a wooden spoon, rub the butter into the crumb mixture until it resembles coarse meal. Sprinkle the topping over the apples, making sure the edges of the apples are covered.

4. Bake for about 45 minutes, or until the top is browned and the apples are tender when tested with a fork.

5. Serve warm or chilled with cream, whipped cream, or ice cream, if desired.

SERVES 8 TO 10

Advance Preparations

Two great things about apple crisps — they are easy to make and they can be assembled ahead of time and baked while you and your guests are eating dinner. Make them up to 1 day in advance, cover tightly, and refrigerate until you are ready to bake. Nothing beats a warm apple crisp, topped with ice cream.

Fresh Fruit Tart

When my son was in kindergarten, I helped in his classroom by cooking with the kids, coming up with a project to match the letter of the week. The highlight of the program was the time we made a tart. The crust was thrown together in the food processor and patted in place by little hands. While the crust baked, we whipped up a flavored cream cheese filling, which we spread on the crust. The children arranged the berries and fruits I had sliced for them, and brushed on a little melted jelly to make the fruit shine. The resulting tart was so beautiful that the principal had to take photographs, and the tart was so delicious, recipes had to be sent home — and all for a dessert so easy to make, even five-year-olds can prepare it.

Butter Crust

- 1 cup unbleached all-purpose flour
- 1 tablespoon granulated sugar
  Pinch of salt
- 5 tablespoons butter, cut into slices
- 1 egg yolk
- 1 tablespoon cold water (optional)

Filling

- 4 ounces cream cheese, softened
- 1 teaspoon grated lemon zest
- 1 tablespoon fresh lemon juice
- ¼ cup confectioners' sugar
- 2 cups berries, or 1 to 2 pounds fresh fruit, such as peaches, nectarines, apricots, or plums
- ⅓ cup apple or currant jelly

1. Preheat the oven to 400°F.

2. To make the crust, combine the flour, granulated sugar, and salt in a food processor. Add the butter and pulse until the mixture is crumbly. With the motor running, add the egg yolk and process until the dough forms a ball. If the dough is too dry to form a ball, add the water and continue processing until the dough forms a ball.

3. Pat the dough into a 9-inch tart pan with a removable bottom, or a 9-inch pie plate. Trim the top edge of the crust to make it level with the rim of the pan. The sides should be about ¼ inch thick.

4. Bake the shell for 10 minutes. Reduce the oven to 350°F and prick the crust with a fork to deflate any bubbles that have formed. Bake for another 15 minutes until golden brown. Cool on a wire rack.

5. To make the filling, combine the cream cheese, lemon zest, lemon juice, and confectioners' sugar in a food processor and process until well blended. Spread over the cooled crust.

6. To prepare the fruit, wash and peel as needed. Slice as desired.

7. Heat the jelly over low heat until liquid. Arrange the fruit over the cream cheese filling. Small berries, such as blueberries or raspberries, can be scattered over the filling. Large berries, such as strawberries, should be sliced. Sliced fruit should be placed in concentric circles, each circle resting on the previous one so none of the filling shows through. Brush the fruit with the melted jelly to completely cover the top.

8. Chill the tart for about 30 minutes before serving.

SERVES 6 TO 8

Advance Preparations

The dough can be held in the refrigerator for up to a week, as can the filling. Rather than hold an assembled tart for more than a day, prepare the components and store them in the refrigerator.

Praline Ice-Cream Pie

An ice-cream pie is greater than the sum of its parts, so don't hesitate to try this very easy recipe. To ensure success, use high-quality ice cream and allow plenty of time. The first time I made this in a home kitchen — my future mother-in-law's kitchen, to be exact — I didn't calculate that the overstuffed, overworked freezer unit atop her refrigerator would be slower to freeze the pie than the industrial freezers to which I was accustomed. Choose two different ice cream flavors for this pie, ones that go well with nuts.

Crust

- 1½ cups (5 to 7 ounces) finely crushed cookie crumbs (Italian amaretti or nut thins recommended)
- 5 tablespoons butter, melted

Filling and Topping

- ¾ cup sugar
- ¾ cup pecans
- 2 pints vanilla, pistachio, or other flavor ice cream, slightly softened
- 1 pint chocolate or other contrasting flavor ice cream, slightly softened

1. To make the crust, preheat the oven to 325°F. Butter a 9-inch-diameter glass pie dish.

2. Mix the cookie crumbs and melted butter in medium bowl until evenly moistened. Press the crumb mixture onto the bottom and up the sides of the prepared dish. Bake until the crust is firm and crisp to the touch, about 10 minutes. Cool completely.

3. To make the praline, line a baking sheet with foil; oil lightly. Stir the sugar in a heavy medium skillet over medium-low heat until sugar begins to melt, about 8 minutes. Increase the heat to medium-high and cook until sugar turns into deep golden syrup, stirring occasionally, about 4 minutes. Stir in the pecans. Immediately pour the praline onto the foil-lined baking sheet; spread with wooden spoon. Let stand until the praline is cool and firm, about 30 minutes.

4. Break the praline into ½-inch pieces. Transfer half of praline pieces to a food processor and process until a powder forms. Reserve the remaining praline pieces for the topping.

5. Spread 2 pints vanilla ice cream gently and evenly in the cooled crust. Use a knife dipped in hot water to smooth the top. Sprinkle three-quarters of the praline powder over the ice cream. Freeze until firm, at least 1 hour.

6. Mound the second ice cream flavor over the first layer, leaving a 1-inch border all around to allow the first flavor to show. Sprinkle the remaining praline powder over the top. Sprinkle the reserved praline pieces over top. Freeze until firm, at least 8 hours.

7. Let the pie soften slightly at room temperature, about 5 minutes. Cut into wedges and serve.

SERVES 8 TO 10

Chocolate Mint Ice-Cream Pie

Ice-cream pies are just about the easiest pies to make, as long as you let the ice cream soften (but not turn into soup) before spooning it into the pie shell, and as long as you let the ice cream harden (really hard) before spooning on the final topping. The final topping will make a smooth coating, as long as it is poured on very hard, very cold ice cream.

Crust

1½	cups chocolate wafer or other cookie crumbs (5 to 7 ounces)
5	tablespoons butter, melted

Filling and Topping

2	pints chocolate ice cream, softened slightly
1	pint mint chocolate chip or other contrasting flavor
⅓	cup heavy cream
2	tablespoons dark corn syrup
4	ounces semisweet chocolate, chopped
¼	teaspoon peppermint extract

1. To make the crust, preheat the oven to 325°F. Butter a 9-inch-diameter glass pie dish.

2. Mix the cookie crumbs and melted butter in medium bowl until evenly moistened. Press the crumb mixture onto the bottom and up the sides of the prepared dish. Bake until the crust is firm and crisp to the touch, about 10 minutes. Cool completely.

3. Spoon the chocolate ice cream into crust. Freeze until the ice cream is firm, at least 1 hour.

4. Spoon the second flavor on top, mounding it in the center. Return to the freezer and freeze until completely hard and firm, at least 2 hours, preferably more. Do not proceed until the pie is completely frozen.

5. Combine the cream and corn syrup in heavy small saucepan. Bring to a simmer over medium heat, whisking constantly. Remove from the heat. Add the chocolate and peppermint, and whisk until melted and smooth. Cool to barely lukewarm, whisking occasionally, about 20 minutes. Spoon over the ice cream, covering it completely. Freeze until completely firm, at least 8 hours.

6. To serve, let the pie soften slightly at room temperature, about 5 minutes. Cut into wedges and serve.

SERVES 8 TO 10

*Not what we have but
what we enjoy constitutes
our abundance.*

EPICURUS

Metric Conversion Chart

Converting Recipe Measurements to Metric

Use the following formulas for converting U.S. measurements to metric. Since the conversions are not exact, it's important to convert the measurements for all of the ingredients to maintain the same proportions as the original recipe.

WHEN MEASUREMENT GIVEN IS	MULTIPLY IT BY	TO CONVERT TO
teaspoons	4.93	milliliters
tablespoons	14.79	milliliters
fluid ounces	29.57	milliliters
cups	236.59	milliliters
cups	.236	liters
pints	473.18	milliliters
pints	.473	liters
quarts	946.36	milliliters
quarts	.946	liters
gallons	3.785	liters
ounces	28.35	grams
pounds	.454	kilograms
inches	2.54	centimeters
degrees Fahrenheit	$-32 \times 5 \div 9 =$	degrees Celsius

Index

Other Storey Cookbooks by Andrea Chesman

The Classic Zucchini Cookbook, by Nancy C. Ralston, Marynor Jordan, and Andrea Chesman. Savor zucchini and other squashes with 225 through-the-menu recipes. Also included are an illustrated zucchini and squash primer and information on how to select, store, clean, preserve, and make substitutions for all forms of the versatile vegetable. 320 pages. Paperback. ISBN 1-58017-453-1.

The Garden-Fresh Vegetable Cookbook, by Andrea Chesman. Take full advantage of the freshest produce every season of the year. Popular cooking methods such as roasting and grilling bring out intensely rich flavors, while new takes on stir-fries, gratins, stews, and casseroles make it easy to add a broad variety of vegetables to every diet. With 275 recipes, this will be the only vegetable cookbook you need. 512 pages. Hardcover. ISBN 1-58017-534-1.

Mom's Best Desserts, by Andrea Chesman and Fran Raboff. Nothing says "home" like Mom's old-fashioned home baking. Here are 100 foolproof recipes for the desserts you've loved all your life with practical advice on how to bake just like Mom does. 208 pages. Paperback. ISBN 1-58017-480-9.

Mom's Best One-Dish Suppers, by Andrea Chesman. Bring your whole family to the dinner table with 101 recipes that satisfy comfort-food cravings with minimal fuss and cleanup. 208 pages. Paperback. ISBN 1-58017-602-X.

Pickles & Relishes, by Andrea Chesman. Turn your bumper summer crops into mouthwatering, low-salt pickles and relishes with 150 simple preserving recipes. 160 pages. Paperback. ISBN 0-88266-744-0.

These and other books from Storey Publishing are available wherever quality books are sold or by calling 1-800-441-5700. Visit us at www.storey.com.